Digging the Deep Web

Exploring the dark side of the web

Pierluigi Paganini

Acknolegment

I would like to thank Rosanna, Alessandro, and Alessia who give me the strength to work hard on cybersecurity topics, sometimes also sacrificing the time we could spend together.

I desire to thank my family, my parents and my brother that are my first supporters.

A special thank to Antonio Iorio and Marco Amabile, they are much more than friends.

Thanks to the tens of thousands of readers that every day visit my blog securityaffairs.co

Special thanks to Julian Hargreaves which is the author of the photo on the cover.

Introduction

The Deep Web, the dark web and too much confusion.

The Deep Web, also known as Hidden Web or Invisible Web, is the portion of the World Wide Web content that is not indexed by search engines.

The term is often improperly used in various contexts, in many cases it is confused with other terms such as Darknet or dark Internet. Before going further in the analysis of the Deep Web and its dark side, it is therefore necessary to fully understand the context in which we operate by providing the definition for each term we will use in this book.

Let us start with the concept of the Surface Web, which consists in the portion of the overall World Wide Web that can be indexed by common search engines like Google, Bing or Yahoo, through the usage of specific applications known as web crawlers.

The Web crawlers are Internet bots that automatically and systematically browse the content of World Wide Web with the purpose of indexing accesible contents.

The Web search engines use web crawlers to update web content, a web crawler could be used to scan and copy all the pages it visits for a successive analysis.

A search engine indexes the downloaded web pages in order to allow users to rapidly get results for their queries.

A web crawler is able to locate and access all the content that is referenced in the web pages they visit, but despite the technique appears very effective for content of interest on the Internet, it misses a lot of material that for some reason is not accesible. We will explore in details later the different conditions that cause search engines failing to index the web content.

The Dark Web is composed by computing systems or computer networks, exposed on the Internet that can no longer be accessed through conventional means. The Dark Web represents a small portion of the Deep Web, that has been intentionally hidden, and the most popular content that resides on the Dark Web is found in the TOR network. TOR users can access to the Tor network only using a special web browser which allows them to anonymize their web experience.

A Darknet is a private network composed of connections between trusted peers through non-standard protocols. The most important characteristic of Darknets is the anonymity, this means that users can communicate each other without being identified. The anonymity represents an element of attraction for criminals, which are the principal users of these private networks.

Example of Darknets are the anonymizing networks TOR (The Onion Routing) and I2P (The Invisible Internet Project) that cannot be accessed with a regular internet connection without using specific applications and software. Darknets are part of the Deep Web because their content could not be accessed by Search Engine web crawlers.

The BrightPlanet intelligence company early 2001 estimated the size of the Deep Web at 4,000-5,000 times larger than the Surface Web, but consider that is a row estimation provided many years ago. Since 2001 the volume of content on the Internet has been increased to an exponential rate, and obviously also the volume of not indexed content has grown. Another factor that must be considered to contextualize the previous estimation is the public knowledge of the Deep Web. Since a couple of years ago, it was a topic known to a limited number of specialists, today the awareness on this part of the Web is increased and unfortunately its popularity is exploded also in the cybercriminals ecosystem.

When someone introduces the Deep Web, he cannot avoid mentioning the most popular metaphor formulated by Mike Bergman, founder of BrightPlanet, to explain this complex concept. Mike Bergman compared searching on the Internet to dragging a net across the surface of the ocean, search engines are able to analyze only the surface of the ocean but there is a wealth of information hidden in the abyss.

In 2001, Bergman published a study conducted for the University of California, Berkeley, which revealed that the overall content in the deep web consists of about 7.5 petabytes.

Which are the scenarios in which the crawling techniques fail?

The categories of content that is not possible to analyze with a classing "navigation technique" implemented by the Internet Bot are:

- Dynamic content: dynamic pages which are returned in response to a submitted query or accessed only through a form.

  Differently from classical hypertext navigation, which provides "static" content (e.g. HTML, XHTML), a "dynamic content" (e.g. Images, text and form fields) on a web page can change, in response to different contexts or conditions. Dynamic content could be realized on server side with scripting technique that modify the supplied page depending on such conditions as data in a posted HTML form, parameters in the URL, the type of browser being used by the visitor, a database or server state, the passage of time.

  Principal server-side programming languages, including PHP, Perl, ASP and JSP, used the Common Gateway Interface (CGI) to produce dynamic web pages on the fly and for this reason are not captured by the web crawler. It is possible to consider as "Dynamic content" also the Scripted content that is composed by webpages only accessible through links produced by a scripting programming language (i.e. JavaScript).

- Unlinked content: as explained, the crawlers inspect the World Wide Web analyzing every link on every single page on their way, but this process fails when a page is not linked by others. On 9/09/13, John Mueller from Google confirmed that the company uses URLs or domain names within content that are unlinked (i.e. Content that doesn't contain a href attribute, to crawl and index new webpages).

- Private Web content: search engines are not able to access web pages protected by any kind of authentication mechanism.

- Limited access content: many websites limit access to their content implementing technical solutions, for example, using CAPTCHAs or Robots Exclusion Standard (also known as robots.txt protocol).

- Non-HTML/text content: textual content encoded in multimedia (image or video) files or specific file formats not handled by search engines.

- Contextual Web: pages with content varying for different access contexts (e.g. Ranges of client IP addresses or previous navigation sequence).

- Text content using the Gopher protocol and files hosted on FTP that are not indexed by most search engines are other categories of web content that are not accessible by web crawlers.

Content and actors in the Deep Web

Let's start debunking a myth, in the deep web it is possible to find exactly the same information present on the surface web. In the deep web it is possible to find licit content, including websites of news agencies, social networks, technical pages and numerous forums on which users participate in open discussions.

Let's introduce the good part of the deep web, every day we read about surveillance activities conducted by almost any government as confirmed by the huge quantity of document leaked by the popular wistleblower and former NSA intelligence consultant Edward Snowden.

Governments ordinarily conduct surveillance activities and Internet monitoring on a global scale, we are all nodes of a global network that exchange an impressive volume of information with peers and machines. The information is power, manage it is the imperative of modern intelligence, no matter if this means hack on a foreign network or distribute a malware to infect millions of unaware individuals.

Snowden has explained how the National Security Agency operates with the help of other Intelligence Agencies, people know that everyone is a potential target, a person of interest, for this reason a growing number of individuals, organizations and various entities are exploring every kind of solutions to preserve their anonymity online. The dark nets, under specific conditions, still allow the Internet users to remain hidden, in many areas of the planet this is a need to avoid the repressive policies of governments, which in many cases endanger the life of innocent people that simply express a political dissent or a religious thought.

But Internet users also escape from private companies that collect every online activity for commercial purpose, an impressive number of firms daily gather information from our presence online. These companies track a specific profile of our habits and in many cases are able to cross data with our sources. Our "surface of attack" is increasing even more, all is started with cloud computing, mobile and social networks, tomorrow we will blame the Internet of Things. All these paradigms have a common denominator, our data, their user-centric vision of the cyber space is fueled by our information and most of the users ignore that someone is collecting their data or that is making profits on it.

The good news is that something is changing, fortunately a growing number of users in the last couple of years have begun to use anonymity networks for legal purposes and to stay away from prying eyes, the most significant example is provided by the Tor network, which in recent years has been used by a growing number of users.

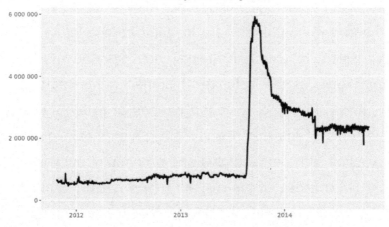

Directly connecting users

Figure 1 - Number of Direct User in Tor Network (Tor Metrics)

Journalists are one of the professional categories more interested in the Dark Web, networks like Tor and I2P are daily used to protect their privacy and security. These networks allow to evade surveillance and censorship operated by authoritarists regime. For journalists it is important to avoid leaving any track of their activities online and dark nets allow them do it.

Deep Web is also largely used by military and intelligence, field agents can use it to communicate each other and with central bureaus.

The Deep Web allows field military agents to protect military interests and operations, as well as protecting themselves from physical harm.

Anonymizing networks like Tor allows military to hide command and control servers for their infrastructure to make them resilient to external attacks. Activists and members of organizations for the defense of human rights regularly use anonymizing networks to report abuses or to fuel the debate on the topic of interest despite the governments discourage this practice with persecutions and a constant surveillance. In June 2014 the rise of the militant group Islamic State of Iraq and Syria (ISIS) was contrasted by the Iraqi government with an online censorship to interfere with the media propaganda of its members. In the country the number of users that adopted the Tor network was literally exploded as shown in the following graph that the number of users since January.

Direct users by country:

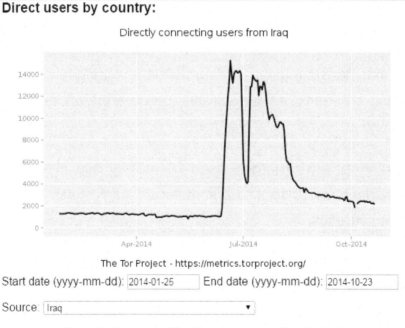

Figure 2 - Number of Tor Users from Iraq (Tor Metrics)

Something similar has happened in Russia, where the Government approved a series of laws which prohibit blogger and journalists to express their dissent against the politics of the Kremlin.

Direct users by country:

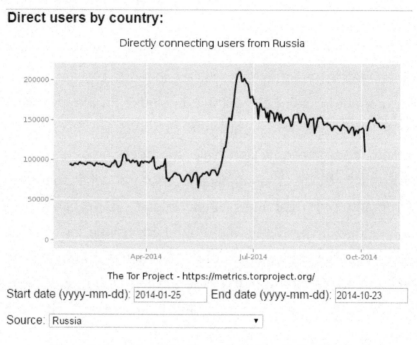

Directly connecting users from Russia

The Tor Project - https://metrics.torproject.org/

Start date (yyyy-mm-dd): 2014-01-25   End date (yyyy-mm-dd): 2014-10-23

Source: Russia

Figure 3 - Number of Tor Users from Russia (Tor Metrics)

Resources in the dark web are very useful also for private businesses, executives may use them to hide company data from prying eyes, for example when the firms operate in countries where local government apply a capillary surveillance. Company could use services and repositories in the Dark Web to avoid cyber espionage and protect sensitive information from cyber attacks.

The Dark Web is full of websites which offer, implementing different models of sale, illegal products and services. Drugs, weapons, stolen credit card data and hacking services/tools are most popular goods offered in this hidden part of the Web.

If we refer the specific portion of Darknets and anonymizing networks it is obvious that the scenario totally changes. The majority of content is related illicit activities and the anonymity of the Deep Web could be easily exploited to provide a secure environment to make a profitable business. In the dark web it is possible to find drugs and weapons, there are efficient black markets specialized in the sale of these products in total anonymity. Black marketplaces offer all the necessary instruments for criminals that intend to propose their merchandise on the web, with mutual advantage for buyer and seller. The buyers could access to trusted communities of vendors and acquire from the sellers with a good reputation, at the same time the sellers could offer their products without the need to build a trading platform.

Statistics

Which are the figures behind the deep web? Let's see wich are the most interesting statistics related to this hidden part of the web. The first data is related to the overall size of the deep web, the glacier analogy probably is the most overused example from the experts to give an idea of the immense amount of information hidden in the hidden side of the Internet.

The statistic more realistic on the Deep Web were provided by Bergman in a study conducted in 2001, the researcher issued a white Paper titled "The Deep Web: Surfacing Hidden Value", published by the Journal Of Electronic Publishing, which is considered a milestone in the study of the hidden part of the web. It has been estimated that The Deep Web contains nearly 7500 Terabytes of information, and it is probably a low estimate, the hidden web has between 400 and 550 times more amount of data than the Surface Web.

Experts sustain that the number of websites active in the Deep Web is more than 200,000 (Bergman, 2001), but the 60 largest websites contain around 750 terabytes of data that is equivalent to ten 10 percent of the Deep Web size.

More recent estimates quantify the volume of the surface Web only at 4% of all Internet content.

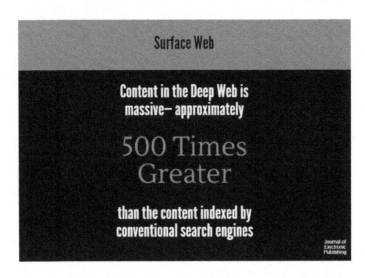

Figure 4 - Deep Web scale (Bergman, 2001)

Bergman estimated that web site in the Deep Web hosts 550 billion documents compared to 1 billion individual documents available on the Surface Web.

It has been estimated that nearly 95 percent of the Deep Web is publicly accessible, this means that users don't need to pay any fee or make any subscription to access it.

Bin He and Mitesh Patel in a study titled "Accessing the deep web" provided a new estimation of the Deep Web scale that is dated 2005, they run a crawling activity that counted nearly 307,000 websites, this means that the Deep web size estimated by the duo is 3-7 times larger that previous analysis.

In 2011 Kunder, Maurice de estimated the surface Web at least 14 billion documents, assuming that the average size of each document HTML is 25k (The Average Web Page 2008), the surface Web would amount to 465 TB. In the

Assuming that the proportion between the size of the Surface Web and of the Deep Web is the same, and it is a pejorative assumption in my opinion, we would get a result of 8 000 – 10000 billion documents that correspond to a total of 186 000 TB – 232 500 TB.

What to aspect from the future?

A growing number of internet users is becoming aware of the Deep Web and they are learning how to contribute to his growth.

The overall volume of data will increase also thanks to growing awareness of the surveillance program operated by numerous intelligence agencies and the need to protect our privacy with the anonymity offered by the hidden part of the web

	Surface Web Size(TB)	Deep Web Size (TB) - Average estimation
Year 2000 (Bergman)	19	7500
Year 2005 (He, Patel)	80	37500
Years 2011 (Kunder)	465	209250
Increment 2000 - 2005	421%	500%
Increment 2011 - 2005	581%	558%

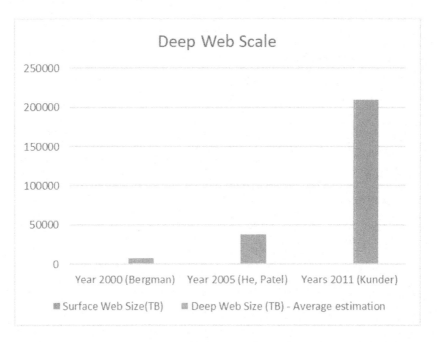

Summarizing, according to the last estimation formulated by the experts the deep Web is over 99% of the Surface Web, the content in the not-indexed portion of the web is the largest growing category of new content on the Internet.

Cyber criminal ecosystems in the Deep Web

Introduction

The analysis of black markets is essential to understand the evolution of phenomena in the cyber criminal underground. The first aspect to consider when dealing with the criminal underground is its fragmentation, criminal organizations specialize their offer for the market they approach, in fact, security experts noticed significant differences between groups operating in different countries. Black markets are the most important points of aggregation for the cyber criminal communities in the deep web, they represent a privileged place where the criminal offer meets a demand even more specialized.

Security experts consider the Russian underground as the most prolific, at least with regard to hacking and payment card frauds, meanwhile the Chinese cyber criminal ecosystem is the most popular for everything concerning mobile frauds and it is focused on the provisioning of hardware for several illegal activities. The Brazilian criminal underground is populated by young criminals specialized in products and services to hit online banking platforms and its users, this is not surprising because of the strong propensity of Brazilians in using the Internet banking. Continuing our tour, we will approach the US cyber criminal underground that presents many similarities with the Russian one, other communities of interest are the Japanese one that is rapidly growing, and the German one that many experts consider a subsidiary of the Russian ecosystem and the Middle East and North African communities. The German cyber criminal underground heavy relies on DarkNets, the most popular forums use mirrors on the Tor Network.

The researchers at TrendMicro who analyzed illegal activities in the Deep Web have identified at least seven different cybercriminal ecosystems operating in Russia, Japan, China, Germany, in the United States and Canada (North America),

Brazil, and North Africa and the Middle East.The Russian underground is considered "a well-functioning assembly line," it is an ecosystem crowded by professional sellers that competing each other by providing goods in the shortest amount of time and most efficient manner possible.

"Each country's market is as distinct as its culture. The Russian underground, for instance, can be likened to a well-functioning assembly line where each player has a role to play. It acts as the German market's "big brother" as well in that it greatly influences how the latter works. The Chinese market, meanwhile, boasts of robust tool and hardware development, acting as a prototype hub for cybercriminal wannabes. Brazil is more focused on banking Trojans while Japan tends to be deliberately exclusive to members." states the report.

Marketplaces like fe-ccshop.su and Rescator that offer products and services for credit card frauds are very popular in the criminal underground worldwide. The Russian underground hosts the most important black markets that offer escrow services or "garants" on their products that make them an important aggregator for the criminal demand, offering a privileged environment where operate anonymously.

"Cybercriminals from every corner of the world take advantage of the anonymity of the Web, particularly the Deep Web, to hide from the authorities. Infrastructure and skill differences

affect how far into the Deep Web each underground market has gone. Chinese cybercriminals, for instance, do not rely on the Deep Web as much as their German and North American counterparts do. This could, however, be due to the fact that the "great firewall" of China prevents its citizens (even the tech-savviest of its cybercrooks) from accessing the Deep Web. The fact that Germany and North America more strictly implement cybercrime laws may have something to do with their greater reliance on the Deep Web, too."

Figure 5 - Underground communities (TrendMicro Report)

The North American underground is the most open to novices, it is visible to both cybercriminals and law enforcement, meanwhile the Canadian underground is focused on the sale of fake/stolen documents and credentials (fake driver's licenses and passports, stolen credit card and other banking information, and credit "fullz" or complete dumps of personal information).

The marketplaces in the Middle East and North Africa are characterized by complete offer, it is quite easy to find malware tools and hacking services, but experts warn that shopping these markets can be tricky for outsiders.

The Russian Underground

Security experts consider the Russian underground the most important cybercrime ecosystem, its operators offer every kind of illegal product and service. According to the experts at Kaspersky Lab, Russian criminal organizations have stolen roughly $790 Million over 3 years (from 2012 to 2015), more than $500 million of that is from victims located outside the Russian.

Individuals, private companies, and financial institutions across the world are the principal targets of Russian hackers. The researchers at Kaspersky estimated the losses by analyzing the information gathered from over 160 arrests of Russian-language speaking cybercriminals as well as data gathered during their investigations. Unfortunately, this data could represent only the tip of the iceberg, in many cases attacks are undetected and it is not easy to provide an estimation of the losses.

"With online financial transactions becoming more common, the organizations supporting such operations are becoming more attractive to cybercriminals. Over the last few years, cybercriminals have been increasingly attacking not just the customers of banks and online stores, but the enabling banks and payments systems directly. The story of the Carbanak cybergroup which specializes in attacking banks and was exposed earlier this year by Kaspersky Lab is a clear confirmation of this trend." reads the Kaspersky's report.

More than 1,000 individuals were recruited by the Russian cyber criminal organizations since 2012, most of them involved in the development of malware and the set up of botnet.

The researchers at Kaspersky have identified at least five cyber gangs focused specifically on financial crimes, typically they are organized structures composed of 10 to 40 people, which are operating for at least two years.

"At least two of them are actively attacking targets not only in Russia but also in the USA, the UK, Australia, France, Italy and Germany." continues the report.

These organizations operate like regular businesses offering a large number of services and products. The Russian underground focuses its offer on hacking solutions and credit card frauds.

"All of these "products" and "services" are bought and sold in various combinations in order to enable four main types of crime. These types can also be combined in various ways depending on the criminal group:"

- DDoS attacks (ordered or carried out for the purpose of extortion);

- Theft of personal information and data to access e-money (for the purpose of resale or money theft);

- Theft of money from the accounts of banks or other organizations;

- Domestic or corporate espionage;

- Blocking access to data on the infected computer for the purpose of extortion;

The experts observed that preferred currencies for transactions in Russian underground include Bitcoin, Perfect Money, and WebMoney. The Russian cyber underground is an element of attraction for skilled hackers and wannabe cybercriminals, this ecosystem offers numerous job opportunities to participants.

How a financial cybercrime group is organized

Kaspersky Lab is actively investigating five large, Russian-speaking cybercriminal groups involved in stealing money using malicious software.

Leader

Virus writer/ Programmer

Head of the money mules service

Malware-packing service

Traffic dealer Spammer Downloads

Money mules manager

Distributors

System administrator Assistant

Money flow manager

Money mules

Server setup

Cash withdrawal

The Money flow manager transfers funds from attacked financial accounts to accounts provided by the Money mules manager. The Money mules manager instructs the money mules where to transfer the money. A share of the stolen money ends up with the Head of the money mules service, while the rest is transferred to the Leader of the criminal group.

© 2015 AO Kaspersky Lab. All Rights Reserved.

KASPERSKY

Figure 6 - Financial Cybercrime Organization (Kaspersky Report)

Skilled hackers are recruited by Russian gangs for malware development, web designing for phishing pages, and testing. A category of individuals that is also requested are the cryptographers, which are hired as 'cryptors' for packing malicious code so as to evade malware detection.

"In general, employees involved in cybercrime can be divided into two types: those who are aware of the illegality of the project or the work they are offered, and those who (at least in the beginning) know nothing about it. In the latter case, these are usually people performing relatively simple operations

such as copying the interface of banking systems and sites."
states the report. "By advertising "real" job vacancies,
cybercriminals often expect to find employees from the remote
regions of Russia and neighboring countries (mostly Ukraine)
where problems with employment opportunities and salaries
for IT specialists are quite severe."

The most interesting studies on the Russian underground
were published by the security expert Max Goncharov from
TrendMicro a few years ago.

The Russian underground is the privileged place to buy
crimeware kits that are continuously updated by sellers to
include new exploit codes. The Russian underground is
composed by an impressive number of forums that offer
products and services, these places are also advertised on
forums in many other countries. Many forums are hosted on
the Dark Web, security experts are observing a growing
number of operators that prefer to use hidden services in the
Tor Network to commercialize their products in one of the
numerous black marketplaces and hacking forums.

In the Russian underground, it is quite easy to find sellers
offering their products and services through the model of sale
known as malware-as-a-service, that means they are available
for rent.

Russian hackers are specialized in the sale
of Traffic Distribution Systems (TDSs) and traffic direction and
PPI services.

Figure 3: How TDSs work

Figure 7 - TDS (Trend Micro Report)

*"In fact, traffic-related products and services are becoming the
cornerstone of the entire Russian malware industry, as buying
Web traffic can not only increase the cybercriminal victim
base, sifting through the traffic stored in botnet command-and-
control (C&C) servers can also help threat actors find useful
information for targeted attacks." states the report published
by Trend Micro.*

Below the list of principal products offered in the black
marketplaces and hacking forums:

- Trojans
- Exploits and Exploit Bundles
- Rootkits
- Traffic
- Crypters
- Fake Documents

- Stolen Credit Card and Other Credentials
  meanwhile list of the most popular services includes:
- Dedicated-Server-Hosting Services
- Proxy-Server-Hosting Services
- VPN Services
- Pay-per-Install Services
- Denial-of-Service Attack Services
- Spamming Services
- Flooding Services
- Malware Checking Against Security Software Services
- Social-Engineering and Account-Hacking Services

To better understand the offer of the Russian criminal underground let's give a look to the prices of the products.

Exploits kit are available for $500-$1000, meanwhile malware source could be paid from $800 up to $4000 depending on the type of malware and the additional modules included in the offer.

Prices for stolen credit card data are highly volatile and depends on multiple factors, including the card origin, balance and expiration date.

CVVs could goes for $3 up to $25, a Card Dump is offered for a price included in $20-$60 and a Fullz (data + additional information like card holder's document) are offered for $25-$125.

Russian Cybercriminal Underground Service Offerings			
Service	2011 Price	2012 Price	2013 Price
Dedicated-/Bulletproof-server hosting • Low-end • High-end • Virtual private server (VPS)	 US$160 US$450 US$70	 US$100 US$160 US$40	 US$50 US$190 US$12+
Proxy-server hosting (per day): • HTTP/S • SOCKS	 US$2 US$2	 US$1 US$2	 US$1 US$2
VPN-server hosting: • With one exit point • With an unlimited number of exit points and traffic • Average price	 US$8–12 US$40 US$22	 No data US$38 US$20	 No data US$24 US$15
Traffic-to-download conversion (PPI per 1,000 installations): • Australia traffic • U.K. traffic • U.S. traffic • Europe traffic • Mixed global traffic • Russia traffic	 US$300–500 US$220–300 US$100–150 US$90–250 US$12–15 US$100–500	 US$200–500 No data US$100–250 US$75–90 US$10–17 US$100–190	 US$120–600 US$150–400 US$120–200 US$50–110 US$10–12 US$140–400

Figure 8 - Russian Underground Price List (Trend Micro)

According to experts at Arbor's ASERT Team, a DDoS attack could be launched by renting a service called booter or stresser for nearly US$60 per day, meanwhile the cost of an entire week is $400. Cyber criminals operating the service also offer a 10-minute test sessions to their clients.

Technically, these services could be sold as would-be legitimate tools for security professionals that need to test the resilience of their infrastructure to cyber attacks or their capacity to support a high-volume of traffic.

The German Cyber criminal Underground

The German cyber criminal underground is the most advanced ecosystem in the European Union, beating known markets as the French and Spanish. A study conducted by Trend Micro analyzed ten big crime forums, some of them holding a registered, active base between 20.000 and 70.000 users.

Marketplace/ Forum	Access	Offerings	Total number of registered users	Active since	Number of active users
Bus1nezz.biz	Closed forum with restricted access	Crimeware, drugs/narcotics	6,200	2011	1,580
Secunet.cc	Security forum with both publicly accessible and restricted-access areas	Hacking tools, stolen account credentials	1,800	2013	650
Back2hack.cc	Security forum with both publicly accessible and restricted-access areas	Security wares	9,346	2008	1,440
German-plaza.cc	Marketplace that requires user registration (username and password are required for entry) but activation is automatic	Stolen credit card and account credentials, server access	Not available	2015	Not available
Crimenetwork.biz	Forum with tiered access	Crimeware, drugs/narcotics	64,000	2009	8,000

Figure 9 - Main black markets and forum in the German underground (Trend Micro)

The German underground isn't wide as the Russian one, but it offers a selection of its best products and services, that in the majority of cases are provided by smaller communities of hackers.

The offer of the German underground includes:

- Malware (Trojans, bank-stealers, and backdoors)

- Drugs

- Bulletproof hosts(BPHSs), to used to store malware components, exploit kits.

- Fake IDs

- Hacked accounts

- Crypting services

What does really make the Germany cybercriminal underground the most advanced cybercrime in the entire European Union?

The answer is Russia, because both the German and the Russian underground forums are full of carding service banner ads. These ads are normally associated with Russian underground offerings, but heavily advertised in German forums.

A good example is "Rescator.cm", one of Russia's biggest stolen credit card marketplaces that is being advertised in the German underground, also "SecureVPN.to" but there many others.

The link between Russian Communities and the German ones is demonstrated by the numerous banner ads present in the German hacking forums that can help marketplaces widen their client bases.

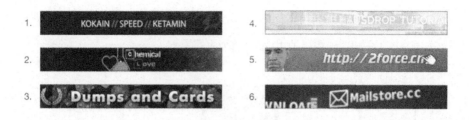

Figure 10 - Banner ads present on the German forums and Black Markets

One of the most interesting services offered by German sellers is the Packstation service described in the report as a delivery method exploited by criminals and that takes advantage of the German postal service.

"Most underground markets rely on droppers who cash in stolen credit cards and online accounts. There is no longer a need for droppers in the German underground. Users instead rely on the so-called "Packstation service" that takes advantage of the German postal service. This allows sellers to put goods sold in publicly accessible metal boxes for their buyers to pick up using their pTANs and access cards." States a report published by Trend Micro on the German cybercrime underground.

The advantage of the "Packstation" resides in the fact that cybercriminals can easily perform "exchange of goods and payment.

Users' addresses cannot be tracked though they need to apply for the service using a physical (home) address and a mobile phone number (which are easy to fake) so they can receive short messaging service (SMS) notifications along with their TANs to claim their parcels"

Get a bitcoin wallet.

Contact the Packstation service provider and buy a hacked account. (Note that there are two types of Packstation accounts—one that is bound to a mobile number and email address and another that is "clear," which means you can use a mobile number of your choice.)

Buy whatever you want (without spending anything) from online shops like Amazon or Zalando that allow Packstation delivery.

Figure 18: How cybercriminals avail of Packstation access

Figure 11 - Packstation service (Trend Micro Report)

I have found very interesting the German-plaza.cc black market, which is hosted on the CloudFlare platform.

The black marketplace proposed a very complete offer that was integrated frequently with new services and products.

Prices are highly volatile, but it is easy to note that they are greater than the ones for products in the Russian underground.

It is likely that criminal organizations are trying to earn from the localizations of many products and services coming from the Russian ecosystem.

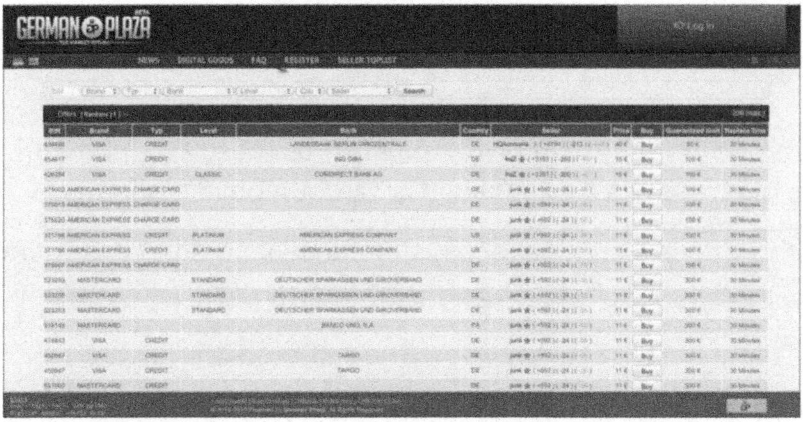

Figure 12 - German Plaza underground Market (Trend Micro)

The main difference with the Russian market is the propensity of the German hackers in the use of Dark Web for their business. German cyber criminals exploit hidden service in Tor network to mirror their marketplaces that are available also on the Surface Web.

Sito Web	Mirror su rete Tor
Bus1nezz.biz	Bizznza4vtgsdrgb.onion
Black2hack.cc	Gerpla4igmngtpgw.onion
German-plaza.cc	Gerpla4igmngtpgw.onion
Crimenetwork.biz	Crimenc5wxi63f4r.onion

The Chinese criminal underground is the most important for the offer of tools and services to target mobile platforms.

In this specific criminal ecosystem, toolkits are becoming more available and cheaper and some are even offered free of charge.

Cyber criminals could buy a crimeware kit for nearly 100 yuan ($15,00) and the selling of premium-rate phone numbers can be bought for 220,000 yuan ($33,900).

Premium service abusers can subscribe mobile users to unwanted services, they leverage malicious mobile apps to reply via text message on users' behalf, in this way victims are charged a subscription fee by the services.

In order to hide their activities, the apps are able to delete confirmation text messages without notifying the operation to the user.

Mobile spam campaigns are profitable activities for the criminal organizations considering that more than 80% of the Chinese netizens access the Internet through mobile devices.

Mobile spammers use to send unsolicited bulk text messages ("SMS spam") to victims' handset to advertise products and services or to spread phishing URLs and malicious links pointing to compromised domains.

The offer in the Chinese underground also includes hardware devices traded that allow crooks to arrange mobile spam campaigns.

The hardware devices available on Chinese forums are:

- GSM modems: devices that can send and receive text messages. A 16-slot GSM modem is available for sale at approximately 2,600 yuan (US$400) and is able to send up to 9,600 text messages per hour.

- SMS servers: low-cost piece of radio frequency (RF) hardware that can send out software-defined radio (SDR) signals in GSM frequency ranges. The cost for a server starts from 45,000 yuan (~US$ 6,934).

- Internet short message gateways: devices that mobile network carriers provide to service providers to handle bulk-text-sending services. A similar device costs 300 yuan (~US$46) for 5,000 text messages and could goes up to 2,800 yuan (~US$431) for 100,000 text messages.

Figure 3: A GSM modem with 16 SIM card slots   Figure 4: An 8-slot GSM modem with SIM cards

Figure 13 - Hardware offered for sale in the Chinese Underground

Another family of malware sold in the Chinese black marketplaces are the SMS forwarder, these devices are Android Trojans designed to steal authentication or verification codes sent via text messages.

Cybercriminal Underground Wares Sold in China		
Product/Service	Feature	Price
Premium service numbers	Can be rented or bought by anyone; can subscribe all China Mobile users to premium services just by sending text messages; comes with detailed subscription reports from network carriers; 15% of the total subscription income goes to the network carrier and the remainder goes to renter or owner	Six-digit subscription number: RMB 220,000 (~US$36,000) per year
		Seven-digit subscription number: RMB 100,000 (~US$16,400) per year
		Eight-digit subscription number: RMB 50,000 (~US$8,200) per year
		Nine-digit subscription number: RMB 15,000 (~US$2,500) per year
SMS forwarder source code for Android	Intercepts SMS from certain phone numbers; removes intercepted SMS from phones; has a hidden app icon	RMB 3,000 (~US$500)

Figure 14 - Chinese Underground Offer (Trend Micro Report)

These malicious software monitors incoming text messages sent by certain phone numbers usually associated with online payment service providers and banks to intercept authentication or verification codes, then they forward the SMSs to the cybercriminals.

SMS forwarders, like premium service abusers, are able to hide their activity by deleting the text messages they intercept.

In the Chinese underground it is possible to pay for spam services via Apple iMessage spammers that could be acquired in lot of 1,000 spam services for as little as 100 yuan ($15,00).

In 2014, security experts at Trend Micro conducted a study to measure the popularity of various products and services offered in the Chinese underground market and they observed that the greatest interest was for products and belonging to these three categories:

Compromised hosts

- Distributed denial-of-service (DDoS) attack services
- Remote access tools/Trojans (RATs).

The report published by the experts includes the price list for the above products, for example an annual license for RAT ranges from $97 to $258, meanwhile criminals could rent DDoS toolkits for $81 per month at the time of the study.

A DNS server attack cost only $323 and a 10 GB SYN packets per day goes for $161.

These prices have dropped over the years and today these products are cheaper.

It is interesting to highlight some differences between Russian and Chinese underground, Chinese groups are more available to general public respect Russians peers. The communication channels adopted by Chinese criminals are rarely hidden.

The Brazilian Underground

The Brazil underground, is becoming popular as the Russian and the Chinese ecosystems. The main actors in the Brazilian cybercriminal underground are unscrupulous youngsters, most of them are young and bold individuals with no regard for the law.

Unlike criminal communities in other countries, they do not rely so much on the anonymizing networks for transactions. They exhibit blatant disregard for the law by the way they use the clear web, in particular Brazilian criminals make a large use of popular social media platforms such as Facebook.

Operators in the Brazilian underground show a great expertise in the sale of online banking malware due to the large use of these banking serviced in the country.

According to a report published by Trend Micro, Brazil accounted in 2015 for 5% of the total number of online banking malware.

Actors in the Brazilian criminal underground can be classified under two main categories, developers and operators.

The developers are individuals with an educational background that turn to cybercrime because it's a lucrative job, usually they are responsible for the design of new malware. Developers typically don't use the deep web as their peers in other countries, instead they advertise their products through social media platforms like Facebook, Twitter, and YouTube and messaging platform like Skype and WhatsApp. Developers are usually young students that are financially motivated.

"One such developer is the notorious 20-year-old Lordfenix2 whom we profiled in June 2015. This computer science student was able to build more than 100 banking Trojans that can bypass Brazilian banks' security measures. This has earned him a reputation as one of the country's top banking malware creators. He supposedly started developing his own malware when he was still in high school and remains an active underground player to date." States the report published by Trend Micro.

The second group of actors in the Brazilian ecosystem is composed of the operators, which are individuals without specific educational background. They are the actors that buy the malware sold by the developers and use them to target the victims. They normally buy the malware from developers via crime-as-a-service model. Operators are the ones that normally law enforcement agencies catch, in opposite the malware developers that are hard to track down.

Which products and services can be acquired in the Brazilian underground?

One of the most popular products in the Brazilian criminal ecosystem is the ransomware, they are offered for sale at USD $3,000, and can use it to target almost every platform including Windows, Linux, Android, iOS, and OSX devices.

Sellers also offer modified Android apps that could be specifically customized to work as data stealer. Criminals use these apps mainly to steal login credentials or credit card info to resell on the black market. When dealing with malicious code specifically designed for the Brazilian criminal ecosystem we must mention the KAISER malware that is able to bypass the authentication mechanisms implemented by the Sicredi's (a Brazilian credit union) through the time-based token system and steal login credentials. Many others financial institutions could be targeted by the same threat, including Banco do Brasil, Itaú, HSBC, Santander, and Bradesco.

Banking Trojan source codes are sold for around US$386 each, the offer allows buyers to modify their code according their needs, they can obfuscate strings, customize the composition of payloads and add crypters and other solutions to evade the detection. Other products very popular are the Bolware kits and toolkits used to create Bolware that are offered for around US$155, the applications offered by cybercriminals are user-friendly and implements an easy to use control panel for monitoring and managing infections and malicious activities.

Brazilian Underground Market Product Offerings		
Product	Details	Prices
Banking Trojans	• Builder • Source code	• R$1,000 (US$386) • R$1,000 (US$386)
Bolware kits	Contain bolware for various institutions that accept boletos as payment	R$400 (US$155)
Business application account credentials	• Unitfour's InTouch • Serasa Experian	• R$400 (US$155) • R$500 (US$193)

Figure 15 - Brazilian Underground Offer (Trend Micro)

The PII-querying services are offered for sale at US$6.81and allow criminals to access PII information included in archives like the vehicle registration plate database, or the CadSUS database (the Brazilian heath card system).

Proxy keyloggers are other precious commodities, they are tools used to redirect victims to the attacker's page, like a fake bank page. Crooks use it to serve malware on the victim's machine and control it.

The "Remota" keyloggers is sold for US$511.61 including full support and weekly updates.

DNS changers are offered for sale in the market for around US$1279.02, crooks used it to redirect victims to a phishing page or to a domain hosting an exploit kit. DNS changers found in Brazil during 2015 were mainly written in JavaScript.

One of the most interesting aspects of the Brazilian underground is the availability of training for criminal wannabes. Brazilian sellers offer all sorts of training courses, including malware development, managing botnets, and stealing credit card data, for around US$51.16 it possible to buy a programming training with online support via Skype.

The Brazilian cybercrime underground currently offers bank fraud courses to aspiring cyber-criminals, the courses are very advanced and propose detailed information for beginners to the criminal activities.

The courses start presenting the fraud workflow and tools necessary to arrange a cyber fraud. Some courses are arranged in modules that include interesting information on the illegal practices to cybercriminal wannabes that can acquire also interactive guides and practical exercises (e.g., simulating attacks). A 10-module course, for example, is offered for US$468, the operators also offer updates and a Skype contact service.

"What distinguishes the Brazilian underground from others is the fact that it also offers training services for cybercriminal

wannabes," according to the whitepaper. "Cybercriminals in Brazil particularly offer FUD (fully undetectable) crypter programming and fraud training by selling how-to videos and providing support services via Skype." States the report published by Trend Micro

"Anyone who is Internet savvy and has basic computing knowledge and skill can avail of training services to become cybercriminals. How-to videos and forums where they can exchange information with peers abound underground. Several trainers offer services as well. They even offer support when training ends."

Of course, products and services for payment card frauds are among the most commercialized commodities, it is quite easy to find stolen credit card credentials, Credit card number generators and so on.

Post Skimmers are normally sold for around US$2046.43, but very useful are credit card transaction approval services and training that assist crooks in using the stolen card in cash out activities.

Fake documents and counterfeit money are other products very popular in the Brazilian underground, priced depends on the type of document and its country.

Crooks can pay to get a new ID card, or a new driver's license.

According to the author of the study of the Brazilian underground market, Trend Micro Senior Threat Researcher Fernando Merces, several factors have contributed to the growth of cyber-criminal activity in the country like limited resources assigned to law enforcement and the existence of a flexible underground market.

"For example, Brazil has a lack of concrete laws and limited law enforcement agency resources that address cybercrime in the country," he noted. "Additionally, the technological and consumer landscape in Brazil, which has a 50% Internet penetration rate, and a 69% credit card penetration rate, has made the country all too appealing for cybercriminals. However, another factor may have also contributed to Brazilian cybercrime: the existence of a flexible underground market with different offerings, ranging from banking Trojan development to online fraud training. The latter is highly notable as this is the most unique item in the market, which may not be found in other underground markets." explained Merces in a blog post.*

Let me suggest you to read the full report published by Trend Micro, it is full of interesting information.

Unlike other criminal underground markets, the North American one isn't so hidden, in fact, criminals in North America doesn't use the dark web. The offer in this specific ecosystem is tailored for US and Canadian operators, most of the offerings (stolen accounts, products and services, and fake documents) are based in the US. In the North American undergroun it is possible to buy several illegal products and services including weapons, drugs, hacking services, passports, bulletproof vests, and even money laundering services. The most traded products in this cyber underground are drugs that reach 62 percent of market share, followed by stolen card data dumps that account 16 percent and fake documents at 4 percent.

Offering	Price
Blue cheese marijuana	US$19 per gram
THC vape oil	US$24 per cartridge
Sharif hash	US$53 per 5 grams
Valium	US$66 per 75 pills
High-quality Bolivian cocaine	US$69 per gram
Methylphenidate (18mg)	US$70 per 10 pills
Clonazepam	US$71 per 100 tablets
MMDA	US$86 per pill
Counterfeit CVS, Walgreens, or Roland prescription labels	US$100 per 3 labels
Methamphetamine	US$136 per gram
Afghan heroin	US$209 per gram

Figure 16 - Drugs offered in the North America Underground (Trend Micro)

It is curious to see that it is possible to pay for a "murder for hire" which provides several options, for example a simple beating goes for $3,000, or an "accidental death" goes for $900,000.

Crimeware accounts for 15 percent of the overall market that includes things like, buying malware, hacking services. The American underground relies on forums solely dedicated to the sale of hacking tools like keyloggers, remote access Trojan and botnets.

A keylogger will sell for $1-$4, a botnet can be sold for $5-$200 and a ransomware can be bought for $10 flat. Many sellers also offer other services such as DDoS attacks and crypting service.

Middle East and North African cybercrime underground market

The Middle East and North African cybercrime underground market has characteristics that make it unique. The listing of marketplaces in this specific area covers every need, it includes products available in any other criminal underground, but experts warn that shopping these markets can be tricky for outsiders. The registration to almost any forum and black marketplace requires a joining fee and the Arabic represents a high entry barrier.

"Our look into these digital souks also revealed how the Middle Eastern and North African underground is not a glass tank like North America's, but more cautious like the French underground." states a report published by Trend Micro. *"Potential customers are barred from window-shopping, for instance, and viewing links or full forum posts requires an account. Registration is a lengthy process that involves paying for one's membership in bitcoins and getting through the language barrier. English-based forums and sites do exist, but there are certain regional variances."*

Researchers also observed many actors offering for free a wide range of hacking tools, malware components, and free instruction manuals. The underground markets in this region are characterized by the confluence of ideology and cybercrime, according to the researchers, there are not profit-driven like other black marketplaces.

Members readily handing out malware tools for free, they tend to cooperate with each other in planning and launching powerful cyber attacks such as DDoS attacks and malicious operations such as spam campaigns.

"Their underground marketplaces aren't profit-driven like Russia's, *or* China's. *There's an ironic confluence of ideology and cybercrime in this region, where the "spirit of sharing" and sense of brotherhood are the apparent forces behind the distribution of crimeware. "* reads *the report.*

"A common practice among its players is to readily hand out codes, malware, and instruction manuals for free. Crypters, *typically used to obfuscate malware, as well as* SQL injection *tools, keyloggers, and basic malware builders, are given away—a reflection of the culture within the regions' underground scene." "The most interesting driver here is the deep permeation of religious influence – from what is sold to how users and sellers interact,"* explained Ed Cabrera, *chief cybersecurity officer for Trend Micro.*

Even if the Middle East and North African cybercrime underground are young it is rapidly increasing, making this ecosystem very dangerous due to future attacks powered by its actors. The researchers also highlighted another worrisome aspect of this specific ecosystem, its players use to have a close interaction with the threat actors in the Russian underground, in many cases, malware coders and hackers from the Middle East and North Africa are hired by Russians.

The research was conducted in the period between July 2016 and December 2016, the analysist from Trend Micro focused their investigation on the kind of merchandise available for sale in these black markets and their price lists. The vast majority of products and services available in these marketplaces is the same that is available elsewhere, such as malware, hacking services, credit card and credential dumps, and stolen identity information.

"The marketplaces are also rife with do-it-yourself kits that provide the resources that even beginners can use to launch their own cyber criminal business. Developers typically sell their malware either as a single binary, or a bundle of binary and builder; and in some cases, access to a command-and-control (C&C) infrastructure." continues the report.

Another element that characterized these black market is the low presence of weapons or drugs, visitors looking to buy these items were directed to forums in the North American underground instead. Giving a look at the price list of the underground offering, markets in this area tended to be more expensive than in other regions. Keylogger goes for $19 in Middle Eastern and North African forums, much more expensive than elsewhere, in the North American underground, it is possible to buy them for between $1 and $4.

Offering	Price
Worm	$1-12
Keylogger	Free-$19
Known Ransomware	$30-50
Malware Builder	Free-$500
Citadel (fully undetectable)	$150
Ninja RAT (fully undetectable)	$100
Havij 1.8 (cracked)	Free

Figure 17 - Malware pricelist in the Middel East and North African cybercrime underground (Source Trend Micro)

The same is for credit card data, as usual, the final price depends on the country origin.

Credit Card's Country of Origin	Description	Price
Canada	Visa/Mastercard	$11–15 per number
	Amex/Discover	$22–28 per number
	Full	$35–50 per fullz
United States	Visa/Mastercard	$5 per number
	Amex/Discover	$8 per number
	Full	$25 per fullz
United Kingdom	Visa/Mastercard	$30 per number
	Amex/Discover	$38 per number
	Full	$53 per fullz
Israel	Full	$33 per fullz
Russia	Full	$25 per fullz
Turkey	Full	$18 per fullz

Figure 18 - Payment Card Data pricelist in the Middel East and North African cybercrime underground (Source Trend Micro)

The stolen credentials and online accounts are also much more expensive, these commodities are very attractive for hackers that use them to access e-commerce accounts and hijack government-owned systems and servers with weak authentication.

The following table shows that the highest price is for PayPal accounts belonging to Israeli users, they go for $50.

Account	Price
Deezer.com account (for monthly service, guaranteed for six months)	$7
PayPal account	$3-10
Israeli PayPal account	$50
Souq.com account	$1-3
Saudiairlines.com account	$4-7
Wadi.com account	$5-8
Windows Server 2008 RDP access	$20-30 (depending on location)

Figure 19 - Account Data pricelist in the Middel East and North African cybercrime underground (Source Trend Micro)

Port numbers for Internet-connected SCADA system were available for free in the criminal underworld in this region, while a WannaCry sample was available for just $50.

Let's close this rapid tour landing into the Japanese underground, which is considered a growing market but still limited in dimension compared with others.

The Japanese Underground has a still highly stealthy underground economy, but criminal activities online are rapidly increasing.

According to the Japan's National Police Agency, the cybercriminal activities until March 2015 increased 40% over the previous 12 months. Japan cybercriminal rings are still newbies, due to the nation's strict criminal laws Japanese criminals don't write malware, in this case severe penalties represent an effective deterrent.

The experts noticed that Japanese Cybercrime Underground is very active in the illegal trade of counterfeit passports, drugs, weapons, stolen credit card data, phone number databases, hacking advice and child pornography.

For example, a US passport, which is normally offered for $5,000-$6,000 by sellers in other black markets, can be acquired on the Japanese market for just $1,000.

Figure 20 - Fake Documents in the Japanese Underground (Source Trend Micro)

Althought the victims of the Japanese cybercrime are mainly located in the country, the researchers observed an increasing interest of Japanese crooks in DDoS tools/services and ransomware, a circumstance that suggests that the threat actors are looking beyond national borders to expand their gains.

Japanese players in the criminal underground exploit secured bulletin boards, virtual PO boxes and secret jargon. The principal payment methods are Amazon gift cards and Sony PlayStation Store codes.

Researchers from Trend Micro reported a case of a Japanese BBS called Tor 2 Channel displaying in homepage a warning that it had been seized by the FBI, Europol, and the US Department of Homeland Security Immigration and Customs Enforcement. In reality, the BBS was active and users can access it by clicking on one of the national flag icons on that page.

"They're building a greater foundation for gilded thieves in Japan," said *Tom Kellermann, chief* cybersecurity *officer for Trend Micro. "These cybercrime forums operate under heavier security than do many of their counterparts in other nations, he says. "Other [nations' cybercriminals] are starting to retrofit operational security. You're seeing them [Japanese cybercriminals] build it from the ground up,""Their number one focus is stealth, remaining covert in their operations and obfuscating their activities."*

In 2014, online bank frauds accounted for $24 million in losses, meanwhile the overall cost of online fraud suffered by Japanese banks was $13 million in the first six months of 2015.

According to Trend Micro, the Japanese banks are a privileged target for cyber criminals, numerous banking malware hit the customers of Japanese financial institutions in the last years.

One of the most popular strain of malware used against Japanese bank customers is Shifu, a sophisticated banking Trojan that has been used to target the customers of more than a dozen Japanese banks. In the following table are reported selling prices for the Japanese criminal underground and the selling prices for the same products in the other criminal communities. At the time of the study conducted by Trend Micro, a stolen Japanese credit card verified by Visa was offered for $60, much more than UK and US cards which cost only $7-8. Prices for PayPal credentials was quite the same in other countries, approximately $1-2 per record. Japan was one of the countries that suffered the greatest number of attacks based on the Angler exploit kit. On September 2015, 3,000 High-Profile Japanese websites were hit by a massive Malvertising Campaign leveraging the exploit kit. Japanese underground still offer such kind of merchandise despite exploit kits popularity is decreased in the criminal underground due to the operation of law enforcement the resulted in the arrest of operators behind the most popular exploit kits.

Country	Selling price	Number of accounts for sale
Credit cards		
Japan	US$14–78 (Average: ~US$60)	207
US	US$2–84 (Average: ~US$7)	126,707
Brazil	US$6–10 (Average: ~US$8)	17,385
UK	US$8–61 (Average: ~US$8)	28,336
Canada	US$3–60 (Average: ~US$16)	36,423
PayPal accounts		
Japan	US$2	7
US	US$2	16,633
China	US$2	37
Brazil	US$2	83
UK	US$2	695
Canada	US$2	274
SSH accounts		
Japan	US$1.40	1
US	US$1.40	1,186
Brazil	US$1.40	16
UK	US$1.40	25

Figure 21 - Japanese Cybercriminal Underground (Trend Micro)

What about the future?

The experts have no doubts, bad actors in the Japan's criminal underground will start investing in the development of their own malware to respond to the internal cyber criminal demand.

"There's far too much talent" for them to not create their own tools, said Kellermann. "This is in line with the cultural manifestation of a lot of people in a society disaffected with the government."

How much is the return on investment in the cybercriminal underground?

Cybercrime is a profitable business and the returns of investments can be enormous, this is what emerged from an interesting research published by the threat intelligence firm Recorded Future.

It is cheap and simple for wannabe hackers to set up their own botnet, a banking trojan can be paid from professional malware developers for $3,000–$5,000.

Web-injects to intercept credentials for bank account goes from $100 up to $1,000, and of course, crooks need a bulletproof hosting that can cost $150 to $200 per month, while payload obfuscation tools to avoid detection can cost up to $50.

Another crucial aspect of the illicit business is the cash out, researchers from Recorded Future reported that there's the 50%- to 60% commission wannabe crooks need to pay from the money you steal from each victim's account if they want it professionally laundered.

The money can be delivered in Bitcoin, Western Union, or other direct methods by paying a supplementary fee of 5% to 10%.

"Once the malware is successfully planted and banking credentials intercepted, the perpetrator has to work with a chain of mule handlers and money-laundering intermediaries to receive a final pay-off." states the analysis from Recorded Future.

"A money launderer with a stellar reputation and is capable of quick turnaround, will charge a hefty 50-60 percent commission from each payment transferred from a victim's account. In some cases, an additional 5-10 percent commission might be required to launder the funds and deliver it to the main operator via preferred payment method, such as bitcoin, Web Money, or the Western Union."

According to Andrei Barysevich, director of advanced collection at Recorded Future, the costs can add up and the paybacks are enormous.

"We estimate the average ROI of a botnet operation to be between 400% to 600%," Barysevich explained.

Which kind of return has the illegal activity?

The returns are both direct and indirect, of course, the main income is related to the funds stolen from the bank accounts, but crooks can also earn selling the login credentials at $100 to $200 a pop, or offering a service of per-demand malware installation on the compromised devices.

The dark web is an excellent aggregator for the crooks, this is the right places where it is possible to find the above services.

Figures like these are driving enormous interest in malware goods and services on the Dark Web.

Researchers are observing that the cybercrime underground is evolving to highly specialized products and services.

A malware for launching a distributed denial-of-service attack can cost $700 and the overall infrastructure for a spam or phishing campaign can run into the thousands.

COST

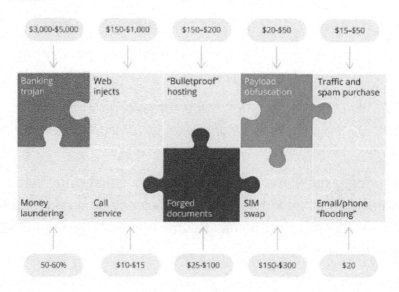

PROFIT

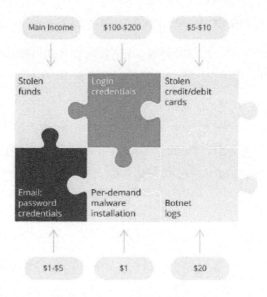

Figure 22 - RoI in the criminal underground (Source Recorded Future)

"The cybercriminal underground is quite verticalized, with threat actors specializing in particular areas of expertise.

It is this distribution of expertise that contributes to the underground market's resiliency.

Similar to drug cartels, once you remove one threat actor or forum, rivals will immediately take its place." continues the analysis.

The underground market is capable to satisfy any need of newbies and script kiddies just as efficiently as it can help the most sophisticated criminal groups and nation-state actors, this is very scaring.

Cyber attacks are rarely conducted by a single individual operating in isolation, any campaign requires expertise across multiple disciplines to maximize the profit ... and any expertise has its price in the criminal underground.

The experts did not observe significant price fluctuations in the offer of illegal products and services in the cybercriminal underground.

"based on experience, we can say a majority of the services and data types have not seen significant price fluctuations," Barysevich added.

CYBERCRIME PRICE LIST

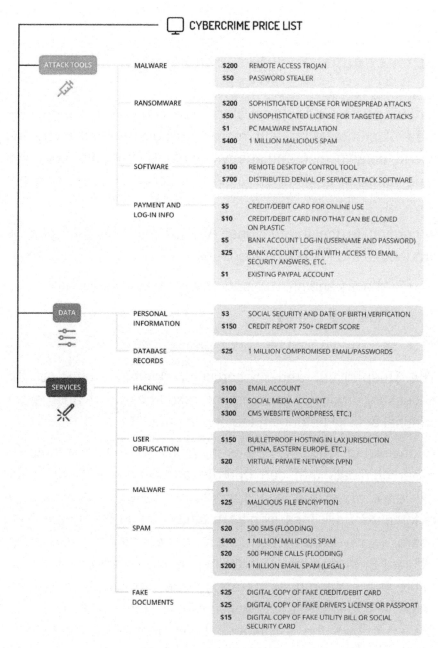

ATTACK TOOLS

MALWARE
- $200 REMOTE ACCESS TROJAN
- $50 PASSWORD STEALER

RANSOMWARE
- $200 SOPHISTICATED LICENSE FOR WIDESPREAD ATTACKS
- $50 UNSOPHISTICATED LICENSE FOR TARGETED ATTACKS
- $1 PC MALWARE INSTALLATION
- $400 1 MILLION MALICIOUS SPAM

SOFTWARE
- $100 REMOTE DESKTOP CONTROL TOOL
- $700 DISTRIBUTED DENIAL OF SERVICE ATTACK SOFTWARE

PAYMENT AND LOG-IN INFO
- $5 CREDIT/DEBIT CARD FOR ONLINE USE
- $10 CREDIT/DEBIT CARD INFO THAT CAN BE CLONED ON PLASTIC
- $5 BANK ACCOUNT LOG-IN (USERNAME AND PASSWORD)
- $25 BANK ACCOUNT LOG-IN WITH ACCESS TO EMAIL, SECURITY ANSWERS, ETC.
- $1 EXISTING PAYPAL ACCOUNT

DATA

PERSONAL INFORMATION
- $3 SOCIAL SECURITY AND DATE OF BIRTH VERIFICATION
- $150 CREDIT REPORT 750+ CREDIT SCORE

DATABASE RECORDS
- $25 1 MILLION COMPROMISED EMAIL/PASSWORDS

SERVICES

HACKING
- $100 EMAIL ACCOUNT
- $100 SOCIAL MEDIA ACCOUNT
- $300 CMS WEBSITE (WORDPRESS, ETC.)

USER OBFUSCATION
- $150 BULLETPROOF HOSTING IN LAX JURISDICTION (CHINA, EASTERN EUROPE, ETC.)
- $20 VIRTUAL PRIVATE NETWORK (VPN)

MALWARE
- $1 PC MALWARE INSTALLATION
- $25 MALICIOUS FILE ENCRYPTION

SPAM
- $20 500 SMS (FLOODING)
- $400 1 MILLION MALICIOUS SPAM
- $20 500 PHONE CALLS (FLOODING)
- $200 1 MILLION EMAIL SPAM (LEGAL)

FAKE DOCUMENTS
- $25 DIGITAL COPY OF FAKE CREDIT/DEBIT CARD
- $25 DIGITAL COPY OF FAKE DRIVER'S LICENSE OR PASSPORT
- $15 DIGITAL COPY OF FAKE UTILITY BILL OR SOCIAL SECURITY CARD

Figure 23 - Cybercrime PriceList (Recorded Future)

Other criminal activities in the Dark Web

As reported by the Interpol the "Cybercrime is a fast-growing area of crime. More and more criminals are exploiting the speed, convenience and anonymity of the Internet to commit a wide range of criminal activities that know no borders, either physical or virtual."

According to the International Agency, cyber crimes can be grouped in the following categories:

- Attacks against computer hardware and software
- Financial crimes
- Abuse (i.e. child pornography)

The Deep Web, and in particular darknets, offer all the necessary products, services and resources to advantage any criminal activity belonging the above category.

Anonymizing networks represent privileged environments for cyber criminals that can operate anonymously. Despite the existence of several techniques to hack the Tor network, law enforcement still face significan difficulties in de-anonymizing users. As revealed by a collection of documents disclosed by Edward Snowden the US intelligence is spending a significant effort in the attempt to de-anonymize Tor users on a large scale. A Top-secret presentation on a project codenamed "Tor Stinks" shows the techniques implemented by the NSA to overwhelm Tor Anonymity with manual analysis.

"We will never be able to de-anonymize all Tor users all the time' but 'with manual analysis we can de-anonymize a very

small fraction of Tor users" states the NSA top-secret presentation.

Another element of attraction for cyber criminal is represented by the fact that the darknets are excellent aggregators for criminal communities. Darknets are places where the cyber criminal communities could could sell and buy any kind of illegal product and services. These places are very attractive also also for the organized crime that needs the product and services provided by cyber criminal rings and lone hackers to conduct illegal activities

Illegal products and services, including drugs, stolen credit card data, weapons, malware, zero-day exploits and fake documents are every day commercialized in the numerous black markets in the darknets.

In the deep web it is also possible to pay for various illegal services, like hacking services, money laundering services and hire an assassin.

Experts at Trend Micro have published several reports of the illegal activities that exploit the anonymity of darknets.

According to the researchers, stolen data is a precious commodity in the criminal ecosystem, and in particular in the Deep Web. The great number of data breaches occurred in the recent months are fueling the underground market of an impressive amount of users' data.

Data breached such as Ashley Madison, OPM and Hacking Team impacted millions of users, their accounts and intellectual property were compromised by even more sophisticated hacks.

The report entitled "Follow the Data: Dissecting Data Breaches and Debunking the Myths" focuses on the data breaches and the dynamic triggered by such kind of events.

The experts integrated their analysis with data from the Privacy Rights Clearinghouse (PRC)'s Data Breaches database, in this way they discovered hacking or malware account for 25 percent of data breaches in Q1 2015. Other causes are insiders, physical skimming devices and the loss or theft of devices (i.e. Mobile devices, flash drives).

Data breaches are phenomena really complex to analyze, it is not easy to promptly discover the root causes neither to predict the medium and long-term effects on the victims.

Some data breaches are caused by threat actors intentionally, others are the result of an unintended disclosure, typically personnel mistakes or negligence.

The statistics on the data breaches confirm that the number of incidents that exposed credit and debit card data has increased 169% in the past five years. It is interesting to note that the value of information in the underground market is rapidly changing. While the prices for credit and debit card, bank account, and personally identifiable information (PII) are dropping due to oversupply, the value of compromised Uber, online gaming and PayPal accounts are rising. PII is the data most likely stolen followed by financial data.

Analyzing the data breaches per industry, it is possible to note that Healthcare it the most affected by these data breaches, followed by government, and retail. The analysis conduced by the experts at Trend Micro followed the entire life cycle of the data breaches, from the intrusion to the offer of the stolen data on the Dark Web. The researchers investigated on the prices of commodities in the black markets hosted in the Tor Network, US accounts of mobile operators can be purchased for as little as $14 each, but the underground offers much more, including Amazon, eBay, Facebook, PayPal, Netflix, and Uber accounts.

Figure 24 - Stolen accounts offered on the Black market

The offer is very articulated and multiple factors contribute to the final price of each commodity, for example PayPal and eBay accounts which have a few months or years of transaction history go up to $300 each. Bank account offered for a price ranging from $200 and $500 per account, depending on the balance and the account history. As anticipated the disconcerting finding of the research is related to the value of personally identifiable information (full address, a date of birth, a Social Security number, and other PII), each record is sold for $1. As already reported by other security firms, document scans of passports, driver's licenses and utility bills, are becoming even more popular. Many sellers in the black markets include in their offer also this kind of information that could dramatically improve the efficiency of fraud schema. Document scans are available for purchase from $10 to $35 per document. One of the researches was conducted by analyzing 8,707 pages considered "suspicious" and examining the "Surface Web" sites that those sites linked to. The experts discovered that the majority of them fall into the following categories:

- Disease vector (drive-by download) sites (33.7%).
- Proxy avoidance sites (31.7%).
- Child exploitation (26%).

The experts analyzed the content and language of the web sites with the intent to figure the possible origins of their users.

The English is the prevalent language for the content crawled by the experts, nearly the 62 percent of website analyzed of 3,454 scouted domains are in English followed by Russian (228 domains) and French domains.

The interesting data are related to the language distribution based on the number of URLs, the number of Russian URL is greater than the English one. The experts motivated this data confirming that some website are mirrored in both TOR and I2P.

By analyzing the principal black markets, the experts tried to profile principal operators, even if the operation is very hard the results are very approximative in my opinion. The analysis revealed that the principal illegal activity remains related to the sale of drugs and chemicals.

"Top 15 vendors across all marketplaces showed that light drugs were the most-exchanged goods in the Deep Web. This was followed by pharmaceutical products like Ritalin and Xanax, hard drugs, and even pirated games and online accounts. This data backed up the idea that a majority of Deep Web users—at least those who frequent the top marketplaces—go there to purchase illicit drugs." states the report.

The researcher discovered many suspicious websites on the Dark Web proposing assassinations services, they included the price list of a criminal group calling itself C'thulhu. The services offered by the gangs including rape, "underage rape," maiming, bombing, crippling, and murder. The prices are ranging from $3,000 for "simple beating" of a "low-rank" target to $300,000 for murdering a high-ranking or political target and making it look like an accident."

Murder Types	Low Rank	Medium Rank	High Rank and Political
Regular	$45,000	$90,000	$180,000
Missing in action	$60,000	$120,000	$240,000
Death in accident	$75,000	$150,000	$300,000
Criple Types	**Low Rank**	**Medium Rank**	**High Rank and Political**
Regular	$12,000	$24,000	$48,000
Uglify	$18,000	$36,000	$72,000
Two Hands	$24,000	$48,000	$96,000
Paralyse	$30,000	$60,000	$120,000
Rape	**Low Rank**	**Medium Rank**	**High Rank and Political**
Regular	$7,000	$14,000	$28,000
Under age	$21,000	$42,000	$84,000
Bombing	**Low Rank**	**Medium Rank**	**High Rank and Political**
Simple	$5,000	$10,000	$20,000
Complex	$10,000	$20,000	$40,000
Beating	**Low Rank**	**Medium Rank**	**High Rank and Political**
Simple	$3,000	$9,000	$18,000

Figure 25 . Black Market price list

The report also confirms the exploitation of resources in the dark web to hide command and control infrastructure of a number of malware, including the Vawtrak and Dyre banking Trojan, and the Critroni ransomware.

Cybercrime is aware of the anonymity ensured by the Tor network and it is exploiting the anonymizing network for several illegal issues.

Banking industry is one of the most targeted sectors by cyber criminals, in particular the number of financial crimes exploiting the Tor network is in rapid growth.

In December 2014, the popular investigator Brian Krebs, obtained a non-public report from the U.S.

Treasury Department which found that a majority of bank account takeovers by cyber criminals, affected banks over the past decade has exploited the anonymizing Tor network.

The non-public report was issued by the Financial Crimes Enforcement Network (FinCEN), a Treasury Department bureau responsible for collecting and analyzing data about financial crimes and fraudulent transactions with the intent to identify and prevent illegal activities, like money laundering and terrorist financing.

FinCEN reported that that majority of bank account takeovers was run through the Tor network, but financial organization still haven't adopted proper defensive measures.

The report, dated December 2nd, 2014, examined 6,048 suspicious activity reports (SARs) filed by financial organizations between August 2001 and July 2014, focusing for those involving one of more than 6,000 known Tor network nodes.

The findings are very interesting, 975 hits corresponding to reports totaling nearly $24 million in likely fraudulent activity.

"Analysis of these documents found that few filers were aware of the connection to Tor, that the bulk of these filings were related to cybercrime, and that Tor related filings were rapidly rising," the report concluded.

"Our BSA [Bank Secrecy Act] analysis of 6,048 IP addresses associated with the Tor darknet [link added] found that in the majority of the SAR filings, the underlying suspicious activity — most frequently account takeovers — might have been prevented if the filing institution had been aware that their network was being accessed via Tor IP addresses."

The most concerning aspect of the report is the rapid rise in the number of suspicious activity report (SAR) filings over the last year involving bank fraud tied to Tor nodes.

"From October 2007 to March 2013, filings increased by 50 percent," the report observed. *"During the most recent period — March 1, 2013 to July 11, 2014 — filings rose 100 percent."*

The data reported in the document is alarming, the three percent of organizations were aware of the connection through Tor network, the Identity Theft (44 percent) and Money Laundering (35 percent) are the predominant types of Suspicious Activity in Tor-related SARs.

Diversity of Filers						
FILER	Money Services Businesses	Depository Institutions - Banks	Broker Dealers	MSB - Prepaid Card Providers	Depository Institutions- Credit Unions	MSB - Virtual Currency Exchangers
SARS	138	133	27	15	3	2
%	43%	42%	8%	5%	1%	1%

Filers Awareness of IP Association		
FILER	Knew IPs were Tor-related	Did NOT know IPs were Tor-related
# of SARS	10	308
% of Filers	3%	97%

Types of Suspicious Activity in Tor-related SARs		
SUSPICIOUS ACTIVITY	# of SARs	Percentage
Other[1]	164	52%
Identity Theft	140	44%
Money Laundering	110	35%
Unusual use of money transfer(s)	78	25%
Account Takeover	77	24%
Unauthorized electronic intrusion / Computer Intrusion	13	4%
Provided questionable or false documentation	12	4%
Suspicious concerning the source of funds	11	3%
Two or more individuals working together	9	3%
Forgeries	8	3%
Transaction with no apparent economic, business, or lawful purpose	8	3%
Suspicious use of multiple accounts	6	2%

[1] A review of Suspicious Activity referred to as "Other" determined that the majority of these activities were associated with Account Takeover and/or Identity Theft.

Figure 26 - Treasury Dept report on Suspicious activity report (SAR)

"Our analysis of the type of suspicious activity indicates that a majority of the SARs were filed for account takeover or identity theft," the report noted. "In addition, analysis of the SARs filed with the designation 'Other revealed that most were filed for 'Account Takeover,' and at least five additional SARs were filed incorrectly and should have been 'Account Takeover.'"

Nicholas Weaver, a researcher at the International Computer Science Institute (ICSI) and at the University of California, Berkeley highlighted that despite traffic analysis could be effective against fraudulent transactions, the approach is unlikely to have a lasting impact on fraud due to the possible exploitation of other anonymizing techniques.

"I'm not surprised by this: Tor is easy for bad actors to use to isolate their identity," Weaver explained "Yet blocking all Tor will do little good, because there are many other easy ways for attackers to hide their source address."

Members at the Tor Project are aware of the significal illegal activities of the Tor Nework and are worried by the possible side effects on Tor users that access the network for legitimate needs.

Fraudulent activities over the Tor network represent a threat to the network itself, traffic congested by botnet activities and the traffic filtering operated by many ISPs, are just a few samples of possible negative side effects for the abuse of the Tor infrastructure.

"A growing number of websites treat users from anonymity services differently Slashdot doesn't let you post comments over Tor, Wikipedia won't let you edit over Tor, and Google sometimes gives you a captcha when you try to search (depending on what other activity they've seen from that exit relay lately)," explained in a blog post the Tor Project Leader Roger Dingledine. "Some sites like Yelp go further and refuse to even serve pages to Tor users."

An Intellectual Property (IP) crime is committed every time someone uses an intellectual property right without the owner's authorization.

According to the Europol, counterfeiting and piracy are the main categories of IP crimes.

Organised Crime Groups (OCGs) are increasingly involved in the violation of IPR and darknets have a key role in the criminal ecosystem.

Intellectual property crimes pose a serious threat to the consumer health and safety. Let's think about the health dangers associated with counterfeit food or pharmaceutical products, substandard clothing, and dangerous toys. IP crime could also affect the environment, counterfeit chemical substances often contain prohibited, polluting and toxic substances.

IP crimes, of course, have a dramatic impact on the revenues of the affected businesses.

The illicit goods and services are increasingly advertised and sold online and the darknets offer a privileged environment to trade a wide range of illicit commodities (i.e. Drugs, firearms, malware, Child Sexual Exploitation Material (CSEM), counterfeit currency, and goods infringing IPR).

Most common products infringing Intellectual Property Rights available on the darknets are:

- Clothes, textiles and accessories (e.g. sunglasses, belts, bags, pens);
- Electronics including mobile phones;

- Jewellery;
- Pirated software (e.g. Adobe Photoshop, Microsoft Office Suites, games, various antivirus software);
- Pirated e-books;
- Pharmaceutical products (especially lifestyle medicines, steroids and hormones);
- Subscriptions to TV channels, music platforms, online game accounts;
- Watches

Officials from Europol believe the growing online trade, including in IPR infringing products, is closely related to the increasing use of parcel and postal services to import and distribute such goods.

Intellectual property crimes are characterized by high-frequency and low-volume traffic.

Experts, trying to link the source of IPR infringing material to specific regions, reported that China is known for counterfeit clothes while India, US, UK, or Canada for counterfeit medicines or steroids.

Most of the IPR infringing products are shipped from Hong Kong, followed by Germany, Netherlands, Poland or Ukraine.

The average delivery time advertised by vendors on the principal black marketplaces was 4-9 work days.

"Criminal vendors sometimes even offered discounts for the next purchase or an extra free shipment should the parcel be lost or seized by the law enforcement authorities. No reimbursements were offered for deliveries to specific countries, suggesting higher risks of seizures." states the report.

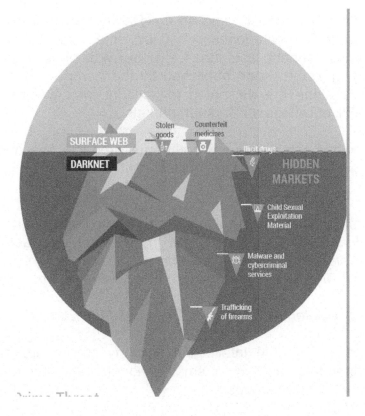

Figure 27 - Dark Web (Europol)

In June and July 2017, two of the largest Darknet markets, AlphaBay and Hansa, were shut down by an international operation, led by the FBI and the US DEA and the Dutch National Police, with the support of Europol other partners.

"Prior to its takedown, AlphaBay, the largest market, reached over 200 000 users and 40 000 vendors. There were over 250 000 listings for illegal drugs and toxic chemicals, and over 100 000 listings for stolen and fraudulent identification documents (IDs), counterfeit goods, malware and other computer hacking tools, firearms, and fraudulent services."

Experts estimated that since its creation in 2014, transactions concluded in the AlphaBay market netted USD 1 billion.

IPR infringing products sold on the Darknet are not grouped into specific categories, usually the operators place them under generic categories together with genuine goods. According to the report published by the Europol, counterfeit products alone are estimated to account for between 1.5% and 2.5% of listings on Darknet markets.

The most commonly listed counterfeit products available on the black marketplaces are counterfeit banknotes and fake IDs.

"The majority of counterfeit and pirated products continue to be sold on the surface web, on major, widely available and trusted platforms, or by online pharmacies. The sellers present them as, or mix with, genuine products, aiming to reach out to a large number *of potential customers." continues the Europol.*

Vendors involved in Intellectual property crimes are mainly lone offenders, trading in small amounts, and members of Organised Crime Groups.

Vendors tend to maximize their advertising profits on multiple Black marketplaces and on the surface web, typically their activity is vertical and focused on a single category of counterfeit goods (i.e. pharmaceutical products or counterfeit luxury goods).

Which are the overall profits stemming from the trade in IPR infringing material?

It is difficult to provide an answer due to the large number of vendors offering different odds on multiple channels. The price for counterfeit goods is typically 1/3 lower than for the original products, the cost reduction can reach about 1/6 of the price charged for the original product when dealing with pirated software or e-books.

The report published by the Europol cited the case of a lone identified vendor that sold large amounts of (possibly counterfeit) Xanax, earning roughly EUR 152 000.

"Some criminal vendors on Darknet markets were reported to have sold on average between 500-1,500 products since they joined the market, with top vendors reaching over 6,000 sales." continues the report.

"Payment is prevailingly done by bitcoin *but other* cryptocurrencies *are also used."*

What will happen in the near future?

Experts have no doubts, intellectual property crimes will continue to increase and darknet black markets will continue to be attractive for both criminal vendors and buyers.

Another factor to consider is the contrast of law enforcement against this specific kind of crimes, that may force crooks to hide their activities in the Darknet.

"In addition, certain measures taken on the surface web against the IP crime, such as frequent monitoring of online marketplaces, may prompt criminals to move the trade into the Darknet. Future trade on the Darknet may increasingly migrate from large marketplaces into new, often smaller ones." concludes the report.
"Illicit goods, including counterfeit goods, will continue to be distributed via parcel and postal services; however, the concealment and shipment methods may become more sophisticated to increase anonymity and avoid detections."

A rapid tour in the black marketplaces

Let's start with the most popular black marketplaces, Dream Market that has been active since around Nov/Dec 2013. The marketplace is available on the Tor network at the following onion address:

http://tmskhzavkycdupbr.onion/

like many other similar markets, it implements a rating mechanism based on feedback and offer the escrow service.

Searching for categories related to IP crimes, it is possible to notice that the category "Other" includes the sub folder titled "Counterfeits."

Under this category, we can find any kind of counterfeit product, including counterfeit currency, clothes, and luxury watches.

Figure 28 - Dream Market Counterfeit products

Exploring the product categories available on the Dream Market we can find also pharmaceutical products (i.e. Viagra, Cialis) for which there is no information about their origin, and anabolic medicines.

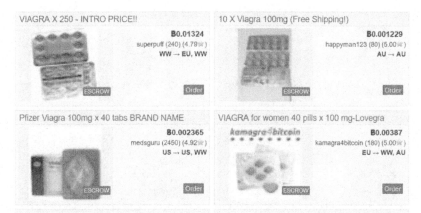

Figure 29 - Pharmaceutical products (Dream Market marketplace)

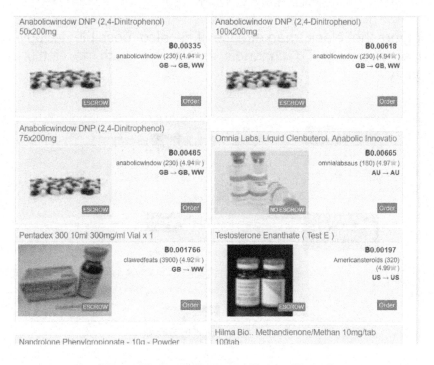

Figure 30 -Anabolic Drugs (Dream Market)

Black markets are the right places where to find also Electronics such as a mobile device (i.e. iPhone) or pirated software (e.g. Adobe Photoshop)

Figure 31 - Mobile phones and Pirated software (Dream Market)

Digging the black marketplace it is also possible to buy a subscriptions to TV channels and music such as Netflix or Spotify.

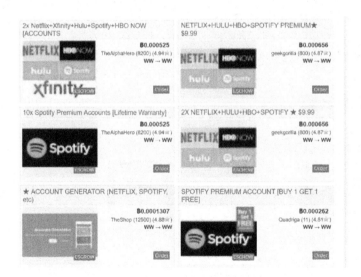

Figure 32 - Netflix and Spotify accounts

Law enforcement worldwide are always involved int the fight against criminal organizations specialized in the sale of counterfeit products.

In November 2017, a joint operation conducted by Europol and other law enforcement agencies resulted in the seizure of more than 20,520 domains for selling counterfeit products.

The operation, dubbed "In Our Sites (Project TransAtlantic VIII)," allowed to seize domains that were offering for sale any kind of counterfeit product, including luxury products, sportswear, electronics, pharmaceuticals and online piracy on e-commerce platforms and social networks.

This is the eighth edition of this global operation against online counterfeiting and IP crimes.

Operation In Our Sites
Project TransAtlantic VIII

This domain name has been seized

Operation In Our Sites-Project TransAtlantic VIII is a
coordinated effort by U.S., European, South American and
Asian law enforcement agencies targeting websites and
their operators that sell counterfeit goods.

Figure 33 - Seized Domain

The "In Our Sites (Project TransAtlantic VIII)" operation was conducted by the Europol in association with the Interpol, the US National Intellectual Property Rights Coordination

Centre (NIPRCC), FBI, Department of Justice (DOJ), and law enforcement authorities from 27 European Member States.

According to the International Trademark Association around $460 billion worth of counterfeit goods were bought and sold in 2016.
"Targeting copyright-infringing websites that market dangerous counterfeit goods to consumers and engage in other forms of intellectual property theft will continue to be a priority for law enforcement," said acting IPR Center Director Nick.

"Strengthening our collaboration with police authorities around the world and leaders of industry will reinforce the crackdown on IP crimes, and demonstrate that there is no safe haven for criminals committing these illicit activities."

Europol hasn't disclosed the list of seized domains that now display the official seals from the law enforcement agencies that participated in the operation.

Below the message presented by the visitors:

"This domain name has been seized

Operation in Our Sites-Project TransAtlantic VIII is a coordinated effort by the U.S., European, South American and Asian law enforcement agencies targeting websites and their operations that sell counterfeit goods."

"This excellent result shows how important and effective cooperation between law enforcement authorities and private-sector partners is, and how vital it is if we are to ultimately make the internet a safer place for consumers. Through its Intellectual Property Crime Coordinated Coalition (IPC³), Europol will continue to work closely with its partners to strengthen the fight against intellectual property crime online and offline." said Rob Wainwright, Executive Director of Europol.

According to data published by the Europol, the agency has seized a total of 7,776 websites in previous "In Our Sites" (IOS) editions.

"A total of 7776 websites have been seized in the previous editions. This year's operation IOS VIII has seen a remarkable increase of up to 20 520 seized domain names that were illegally selling counterfeit merchandise online to consumers." reads the press release issued by Europol. *"This can be explained by the holistic approach which Europol followed with the aim of making the internet a safer place for consumers, by getting even more countries and private-sector partners to participate in this operation and provide referrals."*

Insiders are a dangerous threat for government organizations and private businesses and the darknets offers are excellent points of aggregation for them.

A study conducted by experts at the risk management firm RedOwl and Israeli threat intelligence firm IntSights titled "Monetizing the Insider: The Growing Symbiosis of Insiders and the Dark Web" revealed how hackers in the dark web are arming insiders with the tools and knowledge necessary to help steal corporate secrets.

The research revealed a disconcerting reality, hackers are operating hidden services in the dark web to arm insiders with the tools and knowledge necessary to help steal corporate secrets, commit fraud, and conduct other illegal activities without leaving any tracks.

The researchers focused on the hidden service Kick Ass Marketplace (http://kickassugvgoftuk.onion/) and collected evidence of staff offering for sale internal corporate secrets to hackers, in some cases the unfaithful staff offered its support to attackers to compromise the network of their companies.

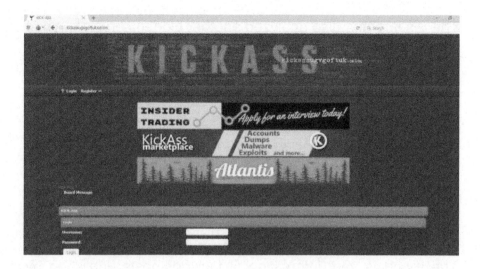
Figure 34 - Kick Ass Marketplace

The research revealed that at least in one case, someone at an unnamed bank was helping crooks to remain hidden in the corporate networks by using a malicious code.

The subscription to the service is of up to one bitcoin a month for access to corporate information offered in various threads.

The administrator of the service, who goes with online moniker "h3x," claimed that Kick Ass Marketplace has seven administrators, three hackers and two trading analysts that check the integrity of stolen data.

Months ago, the administrator claimed that its service boasted 15 investment firm members and 25 subscribers.

According to the researchers, the Kick Ass Marketplace is posting about five high confidence insider trading reports a week that allows the hidden service to pulls roughly US$35,800 a week. The analysis of the associated bitcoin wallet confirmed a total of 184 bitcoins that accounts for US$179,814 at the time of the analysis.

The researchers also analyzed another hidden service dubbed The Stock Insiders (http://b34xhb2kjf3nbuyk.onion) that allows its clients to recruit retail staff as mules to help cash out stolen credit cards for reliably-resellable goods like Apple iPhones.

"Another forum (see Figure 3), called "The Stock Insiders," is also dedicated solely to insider trading. The forum was opened in April 2016. Its objective was to "...create a long-term and well-selected community of gentlemen who confidently exchange insider information about publicly traded companies."

The report is very interesting, it includes posts published by crooks to recruits money mule in charge of cashing out the stolen card data buy goods.

Below key findings of the report:

"By studying dark web forums focused on recruiting and collaborating with insiders, we found:

- The recruitment of insiders within the dark web is active and growing. We saw forum discussions and insider outreach nearly double from 2015 to 2016.

- The dark web has created a market for employees to easily monetize insider access. Currently, the dark web serves as a vehicle insiders use to "cash out" on their services through insider trading and payment for stolen credit cards.

- Sophisticated threat actors use the dark web to find and engage insiders to help place malware behind an organization's perimeter security. As a result, any insider with access to the internal network, regardless of technical capability or seniority, presents a risk."

Insider illegal activities are devastating for the victims, they can fully compromise entire organizations due to the disclosure of company secrets, the weaponizing of the insider is a criminal phenomenon that must carefully monitor.

Unfortunately the condition of anonymity ensurred by the Darknet are attracting a growing number of pedophilies and crooks involved in criminal activities related to sexual abuses.

Three years ago, a group of security researchers published the results of the analysis of such kind of illegal activities conducted in the hidden part of the web. The experts sustain that most of the traffic they have analyzed is driven by activities related to the sexual abuse of children.

Gareth Owen and his team at the University of Portsmouth computer science presented the results of a six-month study (From March until September 2014) that catalogued a significant number of Tor hidden services at the Chaos Computer Congress in Hamburg, Germany.

The experts discovered that the Tor's most visited websites host child abuse images and offer illegal drugs, roughly 80 percent of the visits to Tor hidden service analyzed by the experts were searching for pedophilia materials. According to Owen the number of pedo child pornography websites is over five times as many as any of the other categories of content. According the study gambling websites, propaganda sites, bitcoin-related sites or anonymous whistle-blowing occupy a small part of the darknets investigated.

"Before we did this study, it was certainly my view that the dark net is a good thing," states Owen. *"But it's hampering the rights of children and creating a place where pedophiles can act with impunity."*

The results of the study have created much controversy, especially among supporters of the popular Tor network, who analyzed the result of the Owen's study and offered their interpretation of the research.http://securityaffairs.co/wordpress/wp-content/uploads/2015/01/Tor-Onion_Routing.png

According to the experts that run the Tor Project, the data may have been influenced by the operations run by law enforcement that crowded the Darknets or by numerous denial of service attacks powered by hackers to hit the infamous websites. The Tor executive director Roger Dingledine explained that Tor hidden services represent only 2 percent of total traffic over Tor network.

"Unstable sites that frequently go offline might generate more visit counts. And sites visited through the tool Tor2Web, which is designed to make Tor hidden services more accessible to non-anonymous users, would be underrepresented. All those factors might artificially inflate the number of visits to child abuse sites measured by the University of Portsmouth researchers." reports the Wired portal.

Owen used caution in exposing the results of their analysis, but merely set out the findings of the research.

"We do not know the cause of the high hit count [to child abuse sites] and cannot say with any certainty that it corresponds with humans," Owen resoinded to the Tor Project members.

Dingledine highlighted the importance for the users' privacy of the Tor hidden also referring the choice of the social network giant Facebook to implement an onion version of their platform.

"There are important uses for hidden services, such as when human rights activists use them to access Facebook or to blog

anonymously," Dingledine said. "These uses for hidden services are new and have great potential."

The team ran nearly 40 relay servers that allowed them to collect a huge amount of data on Tor hidden services. The researchers counted more than 45,000 hidden service and analyzed the amount or traffic flowed to them, they also created a web-crawler to explore to websites and classify their content.

The researchers observed that the majority of Tor hidden service traffic, traffic flowed to the 40 most visited sites, was related to the activity of botnets (i.e. Skynet botnet).

Once scrubbed the traffic from the botnet data flaws, the experts observed that nearly 83 percent of the remaining websites were offering child abuse content. Most of the sites were so explicit as to include the prefix "

Several websites were explicitly referring their content, including the prefix "pedo" in their name, of coure the researchers avoided disclosing their names, but confirmed that their content was shocking.

"It came as a huge shock to us," Owen says of his findings. "I don't think anyone imagined it was on this scale."

The study found child abuse websites interested nearly the 83 percent of the overall traffic despite they represent only about 2 percent of Tor hidden services. Black markets selling Drugs and other illegal products (i.e. Silk Road 2, Agora or Evolution) represented about 24 percent of analyzed websites, but the traffic they attracted accounted for only about 5 percent of site requests through the Tor network. Whistleblower websites like SecureDrop and Globaleaks, accounted for 5 percent of Tor hidden service measured accounted for less than a tenth of a percent of site visits.

The study highlighted that the number of Tor users who searched for child abuse materials is greater than the number of users interested in buying drugs or leaking sensitive.

Another interesting data emerged in the study is that most Tor hidden services persist online for only a matter of days or weeks. This phenomenon is quite common in the criminal ecosystem, a technique that allow cyber criminals to stay under the radar, but that gives to the operators less visibility. On August 2014, I have published an interesting post on the technique, citing results on "One Day Wonders" conducted by the security firm Blue Coat.

According to the researchers, less than one in six of the hidden services remained online for the entire duration of the study.

"[The study] could either show a lot of people visiting abuse-related hidden services, or it could simply show that abuse-related hidden services are more long-lived than others," commented Tor director Roger Dingledin. *"We can't tell from the data."*

In June 2015, experts at TrendMicro published an report on the Deep Web based upon information gathered over the past two years by the Trend Micro Deep Web Analyzer. The Deep Web Analyzer is described by the experts of the security company as a web crawler that scan the hidden services and resources collecting URLs of TOR- and I2P-hidden websites, Freenet resource identifiers, and domains with nonstandard TLDs, and extracting content information of interest (i.e. Links, email addresses, and HTTP headers).

The researchers at Trend Micro identified 8,707 pages they dubbed "suspicious" by scanning for "Surface Web" sites that linked to resources in the Dark Web. The experts noticed that most of them fall into the following categories:

- Disease vector (drive-by download) sites (33.7%).

- Proxy avoidance sites (31.7%).

- Child exploitation (26%).

In this case, data included in the report published byTrend Micro gives a different size to the child abuse phenomena leveraging darknets respect to the Oowen's research.

Even if this kind of crimes continues to represent a serious problem for law enforcement worldwide, it could be a serious error to think that they are a prerogative of DarkWeb.

Police from several countries are establishing specific deperments specialized in investigations of child sexual abuses in the darkweb. On December 2014, Prime Minister David Cameron announced that a newborn cyber unit composed by officials from GCHQ and NCA will fight online pedophiles even in the Deep Web.

The National intelligence agencies joint the efforts to track and arrest online abusers and pedophiles. The British Prime Minister announced that the British Intelligence will have greater powers for online monitoring of suspects.

British authorities warned that up to 1,300 children were exposed to online abuse from pedophiles, and unfortunately this data represents just the tip of the iceberg.

Cameron announced the strategy of the British Government at the #WeProtectChildren online global summit in London, announcing the creation of a new unit composed by members from the GCHQ and the National Crime Agency (NCA).

One of the most difficult goals of law enforcement that operate against online pedophiles, is to track this category of criminals that makes large use of anonymizing networks such as the Tor network.

The unit is tasked of investigations related crimes linked to the use of resources in the darknet. Cameron referring the anonymizing networks like Tor said that they act as *"digital hiding places for child abusers."*

"The unit will receive £10 million next year to create specialist teams to find explicit content on the web. There are also plans to criminalize sexual comments sent to children on the internet by adults. The Prime Minister also cited cases in which security services were able to track UK citizens involved in pedophilic activities while using software *designed to protect their identities."*reports RT.com *news portal.*

"GCHQ is using its world-leading capabilities to help the NCA reach into the dark web and bring to justice those who misuse it to harm children," declared Director Robert Hannigan. *"With the NCA, we are committed to eliminating digital hiding places for child abusers."*

Cameron explained that the new unit will benefit of a new technology that allows law enforcement to curb the sharing of illegal photographs and videos online. Additionally, organizations such as the Internet Watch Foundation will assist multinational internet firms including Google and Facebook to identify and block illegal images.

"Every time someone chooses to view an online image or a video of a child being abused, they are choosing to participate

in a horrific crime," Cameron said. *"Every single view represents that victim being abused again. They may as well be in the room with them."*

The opinion of the expert - Maria Laura Quiñones Urquiza (Criminal Profiler - Criminología Forense)

I decided to ask for comment to one of the most popular criminal profilers, Maria Laura Quiñones Urquiza, that was involven in an amazing number of investigation about child sexual abuses.

Which are, based on your experience, the illegal activities that, most of all, can benefit of the Deep Web?

Any kind of illegal activity that takes advantage of anonymity and lack of remorse. In a sane person which is recognized as someone who keeps the coherence, can judge his own actions and keeps contact with reality, committing a crime is a process that involves the conceiving of an action in the mind, then the evaluation if this action gives more economic or emotional benefits than bad consequences like jail or social embarrassment among others, so if those risks are minimum and possibilities are high here comes the decision and its justification that aims to clear remorse or moral structures.

Risk factors as lack of parental control of the risk group of 10-16 years old, exposed to sadistic sex, paedophile content or violence content of Deep Web and even video games could help to develop an adaptive violence, in this case the idea is play the role of an offender of any kind for hours to get a good score in youths that are in the middle of their psychological, sexual and emotional development. Those are real problems because as much as this group sees this content as normal, ordinary and socially accepted (even among a small group), those contents could be naturalized as behaviour. Then becomes violence as an option, not to protect "myself" in front of an aggression or any kind of abuse that might be the natural reaction to defend, this could make violence as an aesthetic way to solve problems and crime as an option for myt frustrations. Some images are so violent and some of them try to introduce bleeding, beaten or brutalized bodies into sexual objects eroticizing them. public exposure of an Industrial secret is a White collar crime that could work on the Deep Web, nobody knows who shares but shares without violence, also how is the best way to abuse a child goes beyond freedom of speech.

Marginality, escape and impunity are some of the important germs that perpetuate and could increase crime.

Is there any proportion between crimes that exploit the surface web and those that explore the deep web?

I have no statistics but as well as deep web has the characteristic to preserve the anonymity for noble and necessary purposes as freedom of speech in countries where this is not a right or share very important information regarding sciences or in my case to appreciate pictures of injuries, suicides, accidental deaths or homicides from the behavioral sciences analysis point of view, and is tremendously bigger than surface web. It's possibilities for crime are out of control or jurisdiction, let's remember that it's also more dynamic than the surface and changes permanently. Personally, I consider deep web a good source of analysis on criminal behavior on the internet because people, for example, who shares pictures of physical punishment on children are also a trend nowadays and what is the impact and answer to this among the viewers is also important in criminology because makes us wonder how spontaneous and honest are their consideration of agreement, disagreement or encourage when their Identification is concealed.

Journalists and laymen of the matter believe that black markets hosted on the dark web are places where criminals can do their business in total security without being tracked by the authorities. They always describe these places as crucial aggregators where it is possible to buy any illegal product and service. According to the media, a keyboard, a few bitcoins, and a couple of clicks allows anyone to buy a gun, an exploit code or any chemical drug. Is it true?

The reality is quite different; the darknets are full of scammers that try to steal money from unaware users that approach the hidden part of the web for the first time. The web is full of users that have paid for products and services purchased on the Dark Web that they never received. In other cases, they have been scammed by professionals that provided counterfeit products.

Let's analyze two emblematic cases that summarize what daily happen to bold users of many darknets and underground forums

Are you searching for an AK47? Read this

The dark web is the reign of scammers; many sellers claim to have products that will never be sent to buyers, even when they have paid for it. Weapons are probably one of the goods that most of all suffer this kind of problems. In the vast majority of the cases when scammers get paid don't ship the weapons explaining to the buyers that law enforcement have intercepted the goods in transit. Of course, victims will never receive the goods and cannot sue the sellers.

A couple of years ago, the producers from the German broadcaster ARD have decided to investigate the possibility to buy weapons on the dark web. They conducted an interesting experiment to understand if it is really so simple to buy this kind of goods, in particular, one journalist tried to buy an AK-47 rifle, aka Kalašnikov and paid $800 worth of bitcoin.

The German journalists were working for a show titled "Fear of terror—how vulnerable is Germany" with the intent to understand how criminals could access weapons offered for sale in the black markets.

The show was focused on the terrorism. It tried to demonstrate that it is very simple to acquire weapons on the dark web, avoiding any monitoring operated by law enforcement.

"There is this experiment at the beginning of the broadcast.#Beckmann Ordered via middleman a Kalashnikov in the darknet.At the end comes out: $ 800 paid – and get nothing." reported the German site Focus.

"Because, as a customs expert, it is not so easy to procure weapons.Sounds weird, but is so.Only that this #Beckmann not nearly as informative as "The program with the mouse."

At the beginning of the show, host Reinhold Beckmann instructed a third party to buy an AK-47 rifle. The journalist also asked to the head of the German Bundeskriminalamt (Federal Criminal Police Office) if it is possible to find weapons online and he confirmed that black markets are the right places where to buy them.

The Beckmann attempt to buy a weapon failed, but it is not clear if the package had been intercepted by law enforcement or it the seller was a scammer.

Figure 35 – Weapon offered on Black Market Reloaded

Searching on Google is it easy to find articles that confirm that such kind of problems are very common when dealing with sellers in the black marketplaces. On November 2015, Joseph Cox from MotherBoard wrote an interesting article to explain the difficulty acquiring a weapon from the dark web.

"One impetus for that is the heavy presence of scammers, who create fake accounts to dupe gullible gun hunters out of their money." wrote Cox.

"I'm just kinda addicted to the scamming part. It's too easy," one scammer told Motherboard in an email chat. The scammer used to operate under the handle "Bartsmit" on AlphaBay, a popular market that sells stolen data, weapons, and drugs, among other goods. Today the scammer is still ripping people off, but under a different identity."

In response to the increased number of scams related to the sale of weapons, several black marketplaces have stopped stocking weapons altogether.

In July 2105, one of the most popular black markets, Agora, stopped selling guns as announced in a statement published by the site administrators:

"Starting from July 15th, 2015 Agora will no longer list lethal weapons.

Following our mission we wish such objects would be available for purchase, but the current reality of it is that the format of a market like ours does not constitute a good way to do it. Shipping weapons is hard; they are expensive and stimulate both scamming by dishonest vendors and honeypot listings by agencies looking to find buyers who might wish to obtain such weapons illegally from us."

Law enforcement warns of a growing number of scammers that operate in the weapon trade in the dark web, on the other side many operators of black markets blame authorities for infiltrating this specific trade.

Besa Mafia, a very sophisticated scam

Many users believe that the greatest risk of acquiring goods in the Dark Web is the possibility of being tracked by law enforcement, totally ignoring that this hidden part of the web is full of scammers.

In many cases, fraudsters offer products and services that are not what they claim to be. One of the most clamorous cases is the alleged hitman website Besa Mafia.

Besa is a term used by the Albanian mafia that means "trust."

The site offers "hitman" services and act as between customers and killers to hire.

Figure 36 - Besa Mafia Website

"If you want to kill someone, or to beat the shit out of him, we are the right guys," reads the hitman website. "We have professional hitmen available through the entire USA, Canada, and Europe, and you can hire a contract killer easily." The group claims to come from Albania.

The truth behind the popular hitman service was clear after the website was hacked and data leaked online. Experts from the Risk Based Security firm analyzed data posted online that includes the lists of "hitmen," photos of targets that the customers had uploaded when asked the service, the overall orders, and the messages purportedly between users and site operators.

"A few weeks ago, one such dark website going by the name "Besa Mafia" became victim of a hacker using the handle "bRpsd," who breached the site's database and posted the

information online where it was accessible to anyone. The information posted is a serious potential *concern as the Besa Mafia site has a reputation as being an actual hitman-for-hire service with links to the* Albanian mafia.*" explained the experts at Risk Based Security. "Data leaked in this breach contains user accounts, personal user messages, 'hit' orders posted to the site, and a folder named 'victims' that contains additional documents within it."The original leak post also contained 250 accounts with usernames, email addresses, and passwords, however, this data was not included in the download. The two CSV files from the leak are named orders.csv and msg.csv that contain 38 'hit' orders and 2,682 personal messages to and from site administrators."*

The experts have no doubt; the website was a scam, and its operators have designed it to maximize their profits considering that murder on demand ranges between $5,000 and $200,000.

The alleged killers have their price list, killing a person simulating an accident is an additional $4,000, beating an individual goes for $500 and burn his car costs $1,000.

The site allows wannabe killers to register their profile on the site, specifying their abilities (pistol or sniper rifle), military background and so on.

In reality, the unique goal for the Besa Mafia site operators is to get paid for services that they are not able to provide.

"These guys have made at least 50 bitcoins [nearly $23,000] on this," said Chris Monteiro, an independent researcher who investigated the case.

In one message from the data dump resulting from the breach, the admin admitted that the site is a scam, and it also shares information to law enforcement.

"This website is to scam criminals of their money. We report them for two reasons: to stop murder, this is moral and right; to avoid being charged with conspiracy to murder or association to murder, if we get caught," the admin writes.

The scammers behind the Besa Mafia were also conducting a propaganda campaign on the web to advertise the services offered by the website and the fact that it was possible to hire a hitman through its platform. Cox explained that someone created a Wikipedia page for the term "Albanian mafia" explaining that the organization was operating a website on the DeepWeb. Clearly the voice was added to advertise the Besa Mafia hidden service, likely by someone of its members.

To increase the reputation of the scam website, its administrators also shared fake information about successful missions completed by the hitmen hired through the website.

They used gory images of murders bearing endorsements for the hitmen behind the site BESA Mafia

"I saw they also have hitmen who do murder for hire, and I was astonished to see that the price was very low: only $5,000," reads one of the messages posted online to increase the reputation of the website.

In February, Monteiro published a second post on the Besa Mafia website, in which he explained that an alleged administrator of the site contacted him requesting a positive review.

Below the text of the message sent Monteiro

"Helo,
I am one of the admins of the Besa Mafia website on deep web.
I saw your blog at http://pirate.london/2016/02/assassination-scams-the-next-generation/
Would it be possible for us to pay for a true and honest, positive review?
Our site is a marketplace, and we have many registered gang members, we are not like the other hitmen sites where they only have one team.
Let me know if we can prove to you that we are legit
Yura
Ps. No PGP key unless you ask for."

Monteiro refused the offer and received numerous threatening messages every time he posted something on the group.

The hack of the Besa Mafia website revealed that the site is a scam, Cox reported the existence of the videos showing burning cars were specifically crafted to increase the reputation of the website.

One of the leaked messages sent by the admins to a wannabe hitman includes detailed instructions on how to make the clip.

"For now, we can use your help to set cars on fire," wrote the admin "Take a normal car, not too cheap or expensive, to the outskirts of a city, write the Besa Mafia URL on a piece of paper, light the car on fire, move back around 10 metres, and show the paper again."

Unfortunately, the dark web is the right place where Besa Mafia-like websites can proliferate without problems. It is quite easy to find bad actors that offer swatting and hitman services on many hidden services and in the majority of cases these sites are backed by scammers.

In the Tor network, it is possible to find also alleged Human trafficking websites, but it is quite impossible to understand if they are a scam because there is no evidence of their activity, but it is also likely that these services are fakes.

Let's close reminding that scammers always try to maximize their profits by selling popular products in the criminal underground such as Skimmer devices and Skimmed Card data or electronic devices such as stolen smartphones and laptops.

In conclusion, the Dark Web is full of scammers and avoiding them is not so easy to novice users.

Figure 37 - Scam Skimmed Cards (Source Stoptorscam)

Card Frauds in the Deep Web

Most of the activities related to credit card frauds are arranged by cyber criminals in underground forums and specialized hidden services in the deep web.

These environments allow to streamline illegal activities related to commercialization of stolen credit and debit card data.

Underground communities offer various products and services, including bulk of stolen card data, malicious codes to compromise payment systems (i.e. PoS, ATM), money laundering services, plastic, and carding on demand services.

In these black markets criminals can easily acquire and sell tools, services and data for various kinds of illegal activities.

The offer of criminal activities is extremely variegated, security researchers constantly monitor black markets and their evolution in order to identify noteworthy trends.

In the recent years, principal actors involved in the sale of payment card data are also offering any kind of documentation that is usually used by crooks in more sophisticated frauds.

Passports, driver licenses and utility bills are commonly used by criminal rings for identity thefts, an activity that allow them to open a bank account or accounts with other payment services, that are used in the cash-out process.

Banking accounts opened with fake identities are used as payment recipients for the sale of any kind of product and service related to credit card fraud.

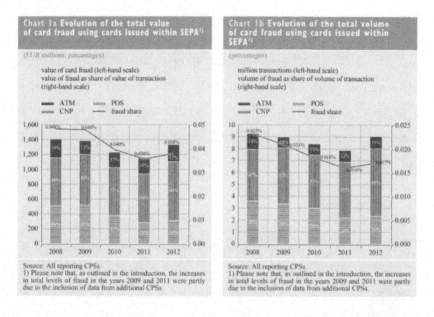

Figure 38 - Card frauds (European Central Bank - THIRD REPORT ON CARD FRAUD)

Another element to consider is that online crimes related to payment cards are becoming prevalent respect to credit card cloning. Criminal organizations that sell products and services related to card frauds in the underground find it more profitable to sell stolen card data than use it by cloning legitimate cards and use them.

These phenomena are strictly depending on the geography, in US where credit cards are still based on magnetic strip, it has been observed an impressive amount of credit card frauds involving malware.

The last years were characterized by an impressive sequence of data breaches that compromised hundreds million payments cards and the Retail industry was the most impacted sector according principal security firms.

The effects on the black markets offer are evident, principal sellers in the underground not only offer stolen card data, but are also focusing their offer for customers that intend to run malware-based attacks against companies operating in the retail industry.

Let's start out tour!

Card frauds - What it possible to buy in the underground?

The credit frauds represent a pillar of the underground economy, the majority of underground markets and criminal forums are crowded by sellers that propose product and services to facilitate, streamline, and industrialize this criminal practice.

Visiting the principal underground communities it is possible to acquire numerous products and services, for this reason let's give a look to the most popular terms used by crooks:

- CVV is a term used to indicate credit card records that may contain several data, including the cardholder name, card number, cardholder address, expiration date, and CVV2 (the three digit code reported on the back of a card). A common error is to confuse CVVs with the code composed by three digits that is on the back of a payment card.

- CCVs are used by criminal crews for online purchase that allow them to cash out the stolen data, the prices for this kind of data range from less than $10 (for U.S. cards) up to $25 (for EU cards sold by sellers with high validity rate).

- Dumps is a term used to indicate raw data stored on the magnetic strip of a smart card. A Dump is usually obtained by physical skimming the card or by using a point-of-sale malware that is able to scrape the memory of payment systems to siphon card data. The Dumps are used by criminal crews to clone legitimate credit cards, their prices depend on multiple factors, including the nation of the cardholder and the card expiration date. A credit card dump cost around $20 - $125, their prices are usually higher of the CVVs because the payoff is bigger.

- Fullz is a term that refers the full financial information of the victim, including name, address, credit card information, social security number, date of birth, and more. The information could be used by crooks to realize more complex frauds, the availability of Fullz allows hackers to steal the identity of cardholders, this means that they could open temporary bank accounts and use them for cash-out. A common abuse of Fullz data consists in performing bank transactions that request users to provide financial information as an authentication mechanism.

- Some sellers also offer Fullz belonging to deceased people, despite they usually include data related to credit cards that are no longer valid, crooks can still exploit them for various kinds of illegal activities. Dead Fullz could be sued to order new credit cards on behalf of the victim, or open a bank account used for cash out though money mules, or for tax refund scams. Dead Fullz usually cost around $1-3 each.

Black Marketplaces

There are numerous places in the Internet where it is possible to pay for products and services related to card fraud, hacking forums, carding forums and hidden services in the Tor network are the places where it is possible to but CVVs, DUMPs and FULLs.

Apart rare exceptions, cyber criminals prefer to purchase stolen credit card data on black marketplaces because these platforms offer escrow services and high reputable vendors are ranked with an efficient mechanism based on feedbacks.

Everyone that searches for stolen card data will find online the name of one of the most prolific carder, the Rescator, which is considered one of the most important players in the underground community that provides any kind of goods related to card frauds.

Rescator manages one of the most popular online marketplace where users can easily buy dumps and CVVs by using a common e-commerce interface. Rascator offers the possibility to choose the product category, the country, any ancillary information like the type of dump (VISA, MasterCard, AMEX, etc.) and the type of card to retrieve.

As shown in the image below, users can also buy card DUMPs filtering by expiration date and banks; this information is very useful for a buyer to acquire data or to use the stolen data to target users in a specific geographic area. For example, the ability to target bank customers in a specific area makes very difficult to discover card frauds with automatic systems because transactions appear as legitimate and goes undetected since the card owners do not report the crime.

Figure 39 - Black Market - Card data sales

As I have anticipated, the anonymity offered by many dark markets in the Tor network is attracting a growing number of seller and buyers.

Every dark market has its specialization, some marketplaces mainly sell products like drugs and weapons, other host communities of carders and hackers that offer many products for card frauds.

AlphaBay was for a long time, one of the best marketplace where to buy credit fraud products.

The AphaBay Market had a specific section dedicated to the Frauds, this category included payment card fraud, account frauds, personal information and generic services.

Before the law enforcement shut down it, the products and services for Payment cards were accounting for nearly 25 percent of the "fraud listing."

Fraud	Percentage
Account & Bank Drops	48,52%
CVV & Cards	19,90%
Dumps	4,60%
Personal Info & Scans	11,70%
Other	15,27%

The black market was offering card data of any country, the majority of which come from UK, US, Australia and Germany.

US stolen sredit card data went for $6-$25, European CVVs were offered for higher prices ranging from $14 to $45. The price of credit card Dumps was higher than CVVs, US and UK collections of data were sold at prices which start at about $ 10 up to $ 100.

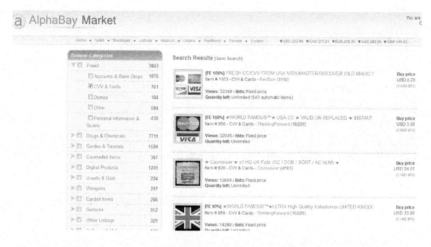

Figure 40 - Alpha Bay CCV listing

There were numerous sellers that were offering FULLZs belonging to bank customers of every country. European Fullz are more expensive respect US ones, their price varies from $15 up to $45 dollars. The majority of CVVs and Dumps relate to US and UK payment cards, US Credit card data costs $6-$18, their low price is a consequence of the availability of a large number of card data compromised in the numerous data breach occurred overseas. European CVVs are sold for higher prices, the most popular marketplaces offer credit card data from UK, France, Spain and Netherlands for a price that ranges from $9 to $25. A limited number of sellers on seeral black markets also offer Relodable card, a precious commodity for card fraudsters that need to cash out their efforts. The criminals use to recharge these cards with illegal profits and cash out by withdrawing at bank ATMs or by acquiring luxury objects and electronic equipment.

Anonymous Reloadable Visa Debit Cards + IBAN bank account [EUR/USD /GBP/PLN]

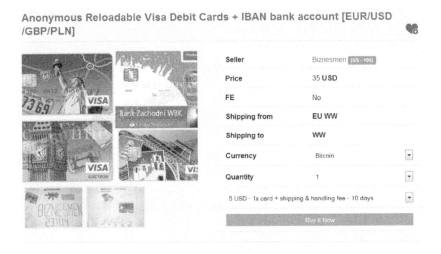

Seller	Biznesmen (5/5 - 105)
Price	35 USD
FE	No
Shipping from	EU WW
Shipping to	WW
Currency	Bitcoin
Quantity	1
5 USD - 1x card + shipping & handling fee - 10 days	

Buy It Now

Figure 41 - Reloadable Visa Debit Cards offered on Nucleus

Another interesting community is the Italian Darknet Community (IDC), it is a small dark market with a good propensity to the carding activities.

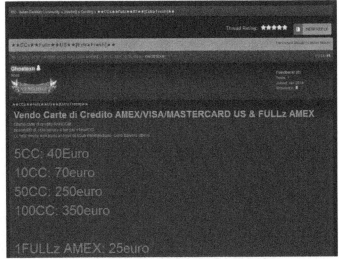

Figure 42 - Italian Darknet Community

118

US Stolen card data (CVV) are offered for prices that range from 5 up to 15 EUROS meanwhile European records are sold for 13 – 25 euros.

A limited number of sellers offer FULLz that goes for nearly 25-45 EUROs for European cards, meanwhile US ones are offered for a starting price of 25 Euros. Among the services offered in the Italian Darknet Community there are also carding and full drop services. Summarizing, the prices for stolen payment card data are extremely variable and depend on multiple factors. The trend in the diversification of the offer relies on the availability of a wide range of services, which can induce a buyer to choose a particular seller. Among these services the escow, the cash out through custom carding services and the personalization of the offer according to various parameters, including geography, minimum amount guaranteed and expiring date of credit card data.

Product	Price
CVVs	
Vista and Master Card CVV (US)	$3-$20
American Express CVV (US)	$5-$20
Vista and Master Card CVV (EU)	$15-$30
Vista and Master Card CVV (Australia)	$8-$10
Vista and Master Card CVV (Canada)	$6-$15
DUMPs	
Vista and Master Card Dump (US)	$20-$45
American Express DUMP (US)	$25-$50
Vista and Master Card DUMP (EU)	$35-$60
Vista and Master Card DUMP (Australia)	$45-$50
Vista and Master Card DUMP (Canada)	$35-$50
FULLz	

| US FULLz | $25-$100 |
| EU FULLz | $30-$125 |

Malware in the Deep Web

Introduction

The Dark Web plays a crucial role in the criminal underground especially for the communities of malware developers, the darknets are privileged environments for vxers and botmasters.

The numerous black marketplaces are excellent points of aggregation for malware developers and crooks that want to trade malicious codes and command and control infrastructures.

The use of dark nets represents a design choice for malware developers that leverages on anonymizing networks to hide the command and control servers.

Just three years ago I made a rapid analysis to determine the number of malicious codes that were exploiting both the Tor network and the I2P dark nets to hide their command and control servers.

The results were surprising, the number of malware that were using darknets was limited, with a prevalence of Tor-based malicious code.

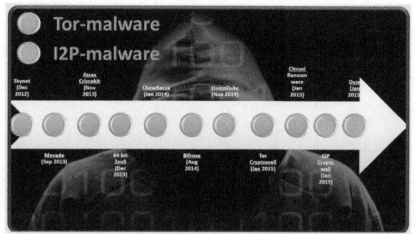

Figure 43 - Malware using C&C in the Dark Web (Security Affairs 2015)

In just three years the situation is completely changed, almost any ransomware today relies on hidden services in the Tor network for the payment infrastructure, many malware are directly controlled by servers hosted on both Tor and I2P and it is quite easy to find Ransom-as-a-Service (RaaS) in the darknets.

Below just a few examples of malware that were discovered in the last 12 months leveraging darknets for their operations:

- 2017 - MACSPY – Remote Access Trojan as a service on Dark web
- 2017 – MacRansom is the first Mac ransomware offered as a RaaS Service.
- 2017 – Karmen Ransomware RaaS
- 2017 –Ransomware-as-a-Service dubbed Shifr RaaS that allows creating a ransomware compiling 3 form fields.

Figure 44 - Shifr RaaS Control Panel

Hiding Command and Control Infrastructure in the Dark Web

Malware authors use to hide C&C servers in the darknet to make botnet resilient against operations run by law enforcement and security firms. The use of anonymizing networks is quite common, but it has pro and cons, let's see in detail which are advantages and problems.

Tor-Botnet

During the Defcon Conference in 2010, the security engineer Dennis Brown made an interesting speech on Tor-based botnets, he explained which are pro and cons for hiding C&C servers in the Tor Network. The main advantages for using Tor-based botnets are:

- Availability of Authenticated Hidden Services.
- Availability Private Tor Networks
- Possibility of Exit Node Flooding

Security researchers use traffic analysis to detect botnet activities and to localize the C&C servers, typically they do this by using Intrusion Detection Systems and network analyzers. Once uncovered a botnet, the security experts and law enforcement agents have different options to eradicate it:

- Obscuration of the IP addresses assigned to the C&C server
- Cleaning of C&C servers and of the infected hosts
- Domain name revoke
- Hosting provider de-peered

The Botnet traffic is routed to the C&C server through the Tor network that encrypts it making hard its analysis.

Brown proposed the following two botnet models that exploit the Tor network:

- "Tor2Web proxy based model"
- "Proxy-aware Malware over Tor network"

"Tor2Web proxy based model"

The routing mechanism relies on the Tor2Web proxy to redirect. onion web traffic. The bot connects to the hidden service passing through the Tor2Web proxy pointing to an onion address that identify the C&C server that remains hidden. The main problem related to this approach is that it is easy to filter Tor2Web traffic, the model also suffers a significant latency due to the Tor network that could make unresponsive the botnet.

Bots implementing this approach run the Tor client on the infected hosts. Bots need to support the SOCKS5 protocol to reach .onion addresses through the Tor network once loaded a Tor client on the victims' systems.

This second approach is more secure because traffic isn't routed through a proxy and it is entirely within the Tor network due the direct connection between bots and C&C servers.

This approach is more complex from a Bot perspective due to the complexity in managing SOCKS5 interface and in botnet synchronization. This kind of botnet could be easily detected by the presence of the Tor traffic on a network.

Strengths and weaknesses of Tor Botnets

The main points of strengths for implementing a botnet based on Tor are:

- Botnet traffic masquerading as legitimate Tor traffic
- Encryption prevents most Intrusion Detection Systems from finding botnet traffic
- The command and control servers (C&C) are hard to localize
- Hidden Services provide a Tor-specific .onion pseudo top-level domain, which is not exposed to possible sinkholing.
- The operator can easily move around the C&C servers just by re-using the generated private key for the Hidden Service.

The main weaknesses are:

- Complexity botnet management

- Risk of botnet fragmentation
- Latency in the communication

The Mevade Botnet - A case study

The Mevade malware (a.k.a Sefnit, LazyAlienBiker) is one of the biggest Tor based botnets in the history, in September 2013 it caused a spike in the number Tor users that reached 5 million.

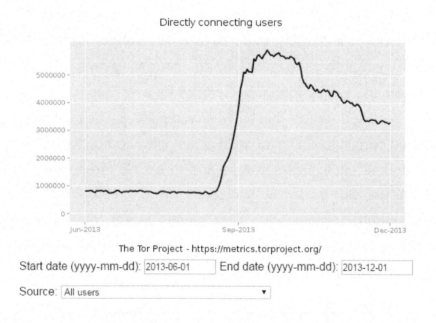

The Tor Project - https://metrics.torproject.org/

Start date (yyyy-mm-dd): 2013-06-01   End date (yyyy-mm-dd): 2013-12-01

Source: All users

Figure 45 - Tor Metrics Mevade Spike Tor Users

Authors of the Mevade bot were Russians, they used the botnet to install adware and toolbars on infected systems, mine Bitcoin and steal sensitive information from the victims' machines. Experts at TrenMicro revealed that the Mavade bot also implemented backdoor features and the ability to communicate over SSH to remote hosts.

Code-signing certificates in the criminal underground

Approaching malware and dark web we cannot avoit to mention code-signing certificates used by vxers to sign the code for malware to evade detection. Some operators in the darknets buy and sell code-signing certificates, but according to an interesting research conducted by threat intelligence firm Recorded Future, the prices for them are too expensive for most hackers. The sale of code signing certificates has increased considerably since 2015 when experts from IBM X-Force researchers conducted an interesting analysis of a phenomenon they dubbed Certificates-as-a-Service (CaaS) and provided some best practice guides on checking for trusted certificates. Digital certificates allow companies to trust the source code of a software and to check its integrity, The certificates are issued by the certificate authorities (CAs) and are granted to companies that generate code, protocols or software so they can sign their code and indicate its legitimacy and originality.

Using signing certificates is similar to the hologram seal used on software packages, assuring they are genuine and issued from a trusted publisher. Users would receive alerts in an attempt to install files that are not accompanied by a valid certificate. For the above resons, malware developers aim to use certificates for legitimizing the malware code they develop.

According to Andrei Barysevich, Director of Advanced Collection at Recorded Future, most of the code-signing certificates are obtained by hackers due to fraud and not from security breaches suffered by the CAs.

"Recorded Future's Insikt Group investigated the criminal underground and identified vendors currently offering both code signing certificates and domain name registration with accompanying SSL certificates." states the <u>report</u> published by Recorded Future.

"Contrary to a common belief that the security certificates circulating in the criminal underground are stolen from legitimate owners prior to being used in nefarious campaigns, we confirmed with a high degree of certainty that the certificates are created for a specific buyer per request only and are registered using stolen corporate identities, making traditional network security appliances less effective."

Cybercriminals offer certificates via online shops, when buyers place an order, the they use stolen identities from a legitimate company and its employees to request the certificate for a fake app or website to the CAs (i.e. Comodo, Thawte, and Symantec). Several vendors currently are offering both code signing certificates and domain name registration with accompanying SSL certificates. The experts at Recorded Future tracked four well-known vendors operating since 2011, only two off them are currently still active in Russian-speaking crime forums.

"One of the first vendors to offer counterfeit code signing certificates was known as C@T, a member of a prolific hacking messaging board." continues the report. "In March 2015, C@T offered for sale a Microsoft Authenticode capable of signing 32/64b versions of various executable files, as well as Microsoft Office, Microsoft VBA, Netscape Object Signing, and Marimba Channel Signing documents, and supported Silverlight 4 applications. Additionally, Apple code signing certificates were also available."

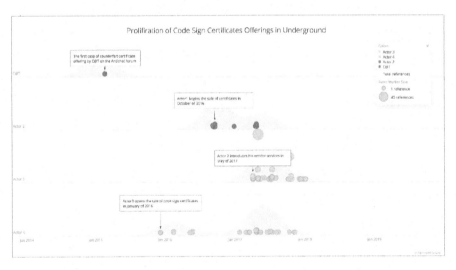

Figure 46 - Code-Signing certificates offering in the underground (Recorded Future)

Prices for code-signing certificates range from $299 to $1,799, most expensive items are the fully authenticated domains with EV SSL encryption and code signing capabilities.

"Standard code signing certificates issued by Comodo that do not include SmartScreen reputation rating cost $295. A buyer interested in the most trusted version of an EV certificate issued by Symantec would have to pay $1,599, a 230 percent premium compared to the price of the authentic certificate." continues the report.

"For those seeking to purchase in bulk, fully authenticated domains with EV SSL encryption and code signing capabilities could also be arranged for $1,799"

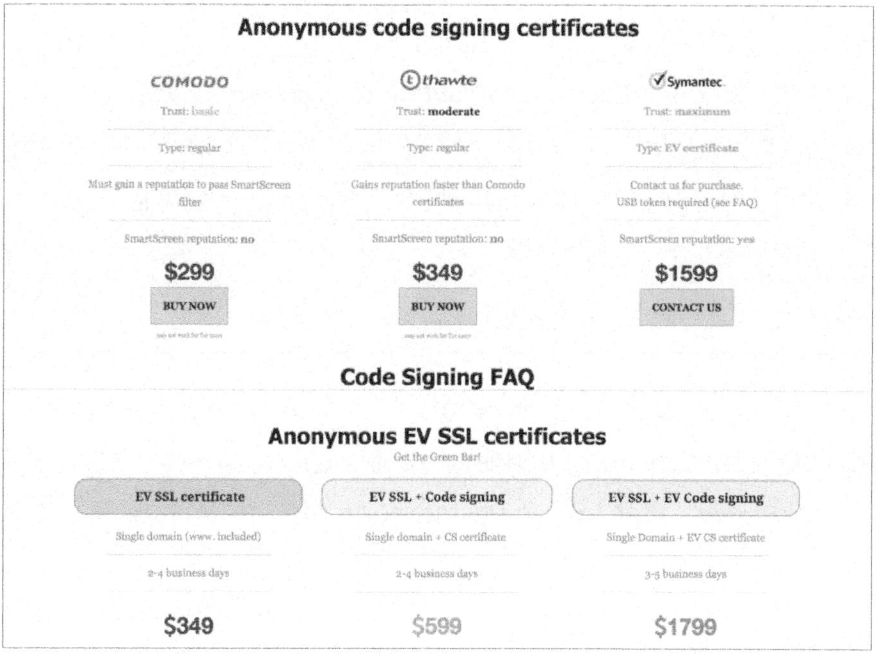

Figure 47 - Code-Signing certificates offering in the underground (Recorded Future)

According to Recorded Future, code signing certificates are not widespread among malware developers due to the high price.

Vxers prefer to pay less for other AV evasion tools, such as crypters (readily available at $10-$30) that represent an excellent compromise between cost and effectiveness

"Unlike ordinary crypting services readily available at $10-$30 per each encryption, we do not anticipate counterfeit certificates to become a mainstream staple of cybercrime due to its prohibitive cost." concluded the report. "However, undoubtedly, more sophisticated actors and nation-state actors who are engaged in less widespread and more targeted attacks will continue using fake code signing and SSL certificates in their operations"

Searching for malware in the Dark Web

In the Tor network it is easy to find hidden services proposing malware and related services to the visitors, below a short list of onion sites that I have visited searching for malware in the last hours:

Name
Anonymous Forum: forum di hackers
Counterfeiting Center
DW - DETECTIVE
Hack Facebook Account
RaaSberry – Ransomware as a service
Berlusconi Market
Dream Market

Wall ST Market
Malware Repository
CrimeBay
MacSpy
Ranion ransomware

Let's start from the Berlusconi Market which has an interesting listing for malware, it includes botnets, exploits, exploit kits and security software.

Surfing the market we can find any kind of malware, from mobile RAT like DroidJack to banking trojan like GozNym. While the android RaT goes for a few dollars, the full version of GozNym botnet that includes the installation on user's bulletproof servers and the code goes for 1500 Euro.

Sellers also offer services for set up a botnet or to power a DDoS attack that is able to bypass protection services (i.e. Incapsula, CloudFlare, Sucuri).

Several vendors offer very cheap Keyloggers (price between 1 and 5 Euro) and DDoS scripts that works also against .onion sites.

The offer also includes various software to hack mobile devices, for example the super Bluetooth Hack goes for less than 3 Euros, it allows you to "hack" into another phone so you can control and access information such as call history, text messages, ringtones, and more.

Let's continue our tour visiting The Dream Market marketplace, its listings is arranged in several categories, some of them include goods that could be interesting for us.

Searching for the term Trojan it is possible to find many sellers offering malicious code, from banking Trojan to ransomware.

Android RATs and info stealers are very cheap, it is possible to buy them for less than 5 dollars. Digging the black marketplace, we can find other malware, like the SMSBot Android bot and BetaBot, both available for less than ten dollars.

Of course, it is also possible to pay for a ransomware, the quality of the code offered on the market is not so good, but this is normal for generic marketplaces.

Figure 48 - The Dream Market - Searching for Ransomware

Another black marketplace that has an interesting malware offer is the "Wall ST Market," it includes specific sections where to find malicious codes, botnets, exploit kits.

Wannabe crooks can buy the ATM Cutlet Maker malware for around $3500, it was first spotted in October 2017 by researchers at Kaspersky Lab that noticed a forum post advertising the malicious code.

A silent Monero Miner Builder could be paid 300 Euro while a Jigsaw Ransomware is available for 120 Euro. Android spyware are very cheap, the DroidJack Android RAT is available for just one dollar.

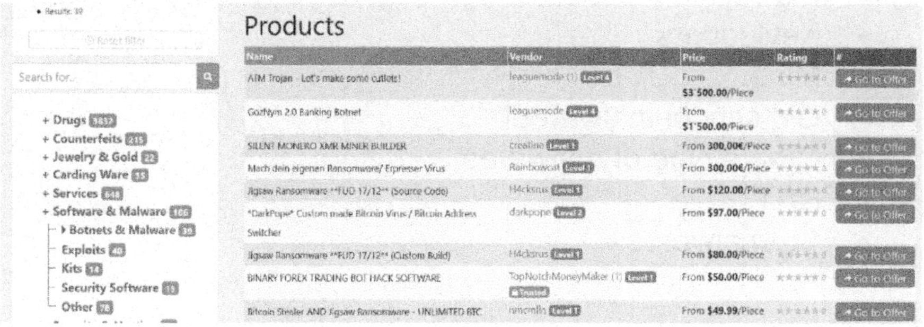

Figure 49 - Wall ST Market black marketplace

On the Tor Network it is also possible to find entire repositories of malware, one of them is Darkoder. Such kind of repositories are well organized and includes almost any kind of malware and component for malware development. Of course, the offer is for more skilled professionals that once obtained the malicious code can customize the installation and deliver them.

Figure 50 - Darkoder Repository

The repository is organized in several categories that includes:

- Botnets
- Crypters
- DOSer
- Keyloggers
- Miner
- Old school malwares
- Others type of malwares
- RAT
- SE malwares

Exploring the RAT folder, we can find popular malware such as DarkCometRAT5, the ProtonRAT, and PurpleRat.

The botnet folder includes several items, such as Banking botnets, DDOS botnets and Logger Botnets.

Searching for Ransomware-As-A-Service I have found RaaSberry, a set of customized ransomware packages that are ready to distribute.

The packages are pre-compiled with a Bitcoin address provided by the users. As any other RaaS, the RaaSberry also provide a Command and Control (C&C) Center to manage your victims and view individual AES keys.

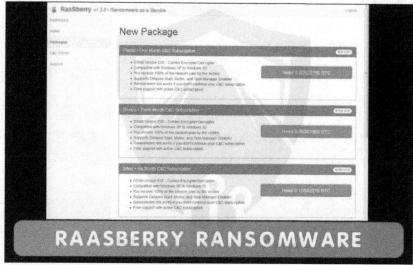

Figure 51 - RaaSberry Ransomware-as-aService

Conclusion

Security experts have highlighted the deep differences between the various black markets, crooks in each geographic area specialize their offer. Brazilian crime communities for example are more focused on banking Trojan meanwhile Chinese hacking communities are focused on mobile malware.

The prices for malware are very different for specific geographic areas.

Giving a look at the price list collected by security firms we can see that specific products in some markets tend to be more expensive than in other regions.

This is the case of Keyloggers in the Middle Eastern and North African forums that are offered on average for goes $19, much more expensive than elsewhere. In the North American underground, for example, it is possible to buy them for between $1 and $4.

Offering	Price
Worm	$1-12
Keylogger	Free-$19
Known Ransomware	$30-50
Malware Builder	Free-$500
Citadel (fully undetectable)	$150
Ninja RAT (fully undetectable)	$100
Havij 1.8 (cracked)	Free

Figure 52 - The Middle Eastern and North African Underground (Trend Micro Report)

The above differences demonstrate the intense activity of malware communities in different regions, their evolutions are often related to the specific habits of potential victims in the area instead of a global trend.

Terrorists in dark web

Introduction

Some studies conducted by independent researchers and government agencies analyzed possible abuse of anonimizing networks by terrorist organizations.

Law enforcement and intelligence agencies fear that the rise of the Islamic State and other terrorist organizations wolrdwide will be associated with an increasing use of the anonymizing networks that makes hard investigations.

The Dark Web is difficult to monitor for intelligence agencies and it is not so easy to locate members of terrorist organizations like the ISIS that share propaganda content.

In the black markets hosted on the deep web it is possible to purchase any kind of illegal product and service, but terrorists used it to share propagana material and initially as a distribution channel for mobile apps used by the jihadists to communicate securely and to transfer Bitcoins to terrorist cells in every place of the world.

A few hours after the Paris attack on November 13, 2015, attacks in Paris, security experts found in the Tor Network a new propaganda hub, a hidden service was set up to share a multi-language declaration (English, Turkish, and Russian) of IS members claiming responsibility for the attack.

The hidden service was discovered by the popular researcher Scot Terban (aka @krypt3ia), who reported it to the colleagues at Salted HASH.

The content included in the hidden service confirmed that the IS were searching for new places on the Internet where share propaganda message without being trcked.

The terrorists decided to move on the Darknet to make the Daesh resilient to take over operated by authorities.

Figure 53 - IS Hidden Service set up after the Paris Attack

According to the study conducted by Daniel Moore & Thomas Rid, and titled "Cryptopolitik and the Darknet," terrorists and radical groups heavily rely on darknets.

The researchers developed a web crawler that was used to analyze and classify about 300,000 hidden services on the Tor network. Below the results shared by the researchers:

Figure 2. **Classification**

Category	Websites
None	2,482
Other	1,021
Drugs	423
Finance	327
Other illicit	198
Unknown	155
Extremism	140
Illegitimate pornography	122
Nexus	118
Hacking	96
Social	64
Arms	42
Violence	17
Total	5,205
Total active	2,723
Total illicit	1,547

Figure 54 - Tor Network crawling

The dark web host a significant portion of services used by criminal organizations to offer their products and services, including "drugs, illicit finance and pornography involving violence, children and animals." 1,547 of the 2,723 active sites of the dark web analyzed by the researchers were used for illicit services, only 140 included extremism content.

The experts concluded that terrorists prefer to share propaganda content on the Surface Web in order to reach a wider audience composed of wannabe terrorists and the curious interested in the activity of radical groups. The two reseachers also highlighted that anonymizing networks are not stable and often very slow.

This doesn't mean that terrorists don't use the dark nets, anonymizing networks have an important role for these organizations, but to maximize online propaganda the Surface Web is the privileged choice.

"The darknet's propaganda reach is starkly limited, not least because novices may be deterred by taking an 'illicit' step early on, as opposed to simple, curious Googling. Hidden services, secondly, are often not stable or accessible enough for efficient communication; other platforms seem to meet communication needs elegantly. Islamic militants do commonly use the Tor browser on the open internet, however, for added anonymity." states the study.

The jihadists communities in the dark web are not very active, in fact at the time of their reseach it is very difficult to find extremist content on the dark web forums.

"One noteworthy finding was our confirmation of the near-absence of Islamic extremism on Tor hidden services, with fewer than a handful of active sites," states the study.

Terrorists organizations today use instant messaging applications for both propaganda and recruiting, these platforms maxime their efforts making very difficult the contrast to such kind of activities on a large scale.

Hunting terrorist in the Dark Web

Izumi Nakamitsu, chief of UN's Disarmament Affairs stated that the dark web is a primary enabler of easing access to WMDs.

Terrorist groups can now trade and collaborate over the dark web and make illegal dealings without being noticed by authorities.

Nakamitsu's declaration highlights the fear that this part of the web could be used by terrorists for different purposes and urges governments to monitor the activities to acoid serious problems.

Pseudo-anonymity condition offered by darknets makes allows terrorists to conduct the following activities:

- Propaganda
- Purchasing weapons
- Purchasing stolen card data
- Counterfeit documents
- Recruiting
- Download Mobile Apps used for secure communications
- Purchase of malicious code
- Fund-raising
- Doxing

The availability of tool and exploits in the criminal underground makes it easy for terrorists to hit computer networks and infrastructure worldwide.

In the last couple of years, some governments decided to respond the IS threat by establishing specific groups of cyber experts focused on terrorism.

On August 2016, the German government announced the creation of a new cyber security unit composed of around 400 civil servants.

"The move is part of a list of measures to boost security in response to recent terror attacks that raised deep concerns about Germany's vulnerability to Islamist violence." reads a blog post published on the GlobalGovernmentForum.com.

The cyber unit named the Central Office for Information in Security Sphere ('Zentrale Stelle für Informationstechnik im Sicherheitsbereich (ZITiS)), supports German security agencies by developing "methods, products, and strategies to fight criminality and terrorism on the internet."

Among the tasks assigned to ZITiS there is also the monitoring of the Dark Web, the experts are concerned about the abuses of Darknets, terrorists could use them to cover communications or to acquire illegal weapons.

In September 2017, the UK National Crime Agency (NCA) started a recuitment campaign for cyber experts and dark web analysts that are hired to investigate illicit activities and dismantle drug rings and dark web marketplaces.

The NCA is investing to improve its abilities to investigating illegal activities in the dark web, on August, the UK agency was searching for a G5 Armed Surveillance Investigator in the Armed Operations Unit, working for the Intelligence and Operations Directorate. It offered a salary of £33,850.

"We are leading the UK's fight to cut serious and organised crime – intelligence development allows us to build a comprehensive understanding of complex and varied threats such as firearms, the sexual abuse of children, people smuggling, drugs trafficking, economic and cyber crime." said a spokesman for the NCA.

"Be they career criminals, professional enablers or those who lurk on the dark web, we will disrupt and bring offenders to justice. Our education campaigns are helping to change behaviour"

The greatest concern for UK Government is the propaganda in the dark web, the National Counter Terrorism Policing Network warned that visiting the dark web marketplaces could be considered by the law enforcement as a sign of terrorism.

Online communities hidden in the darknets play a significant role in radicalization, for this reason, the UK law enforcement focused its efforts also on this specific part of the web.

In a wake of terror attacks in the, London authorities are conducting various initiatives to fight the terrrosim. The police arrested several suspects, but the most curious initiative is the distribution of leaflets with listings of suspicious activities that are to be interpreted by the authorities as a sign of potential terrorism.

"Be aware of what is going on around you—of anything that strikes you as different or unusual, or anyone that you feel is acting suspiciously—it could be someone you know or even someone or something you notice when you are out and about that doesn't feel quite right," reads the leaflet.

Figure 55 - London police distributes a leaflet

Online communities play a significant role in radicalization, for this reason, the police decided to distribute the leaflet.

The listings include the item "visiting the Darkweb," the authorities fear that terrorists and sympathizers could access darknet for propaganda, to smuggle weapons, and to raise funds.

The Dutch police confirmed that the situation in the country is very worrisome, according to a national threat assessment report published by the Dutch police on June 1, the trade of weapons on the darknet is increased.

According to the experts it is always easier to get a rifle than a pistol in the darkweb, law enforcement in the Netherlands seized hundreds of firearms in a few weeks.

According to the European authorities, Holland seems to be a hub in a network of international arms smugglers.

The use of Darknet in well known to law enforcement, some governments created specific units to infiltrate communities and prevent abuses.

Early 2016, the Europol announced a new European counter-terrorism centre to fight the terrorism.

In November 2015, the GCHQ and NCA joined forces to fight illegal activities in the Dark Web and formed a new unit called the Joint Operations Cell (JOC).

In 2016, Bernard Cazeneuve, the Internal Affairs minister in France, said at a National Assembly meeting that the Darknet are abused by terrorist organizations for their outrageous activities.

"ISIL's activities on the Surface Web are now being monitored closely, and the decision by a number of governments to take down or filter extremist content has forced the jihadists to look for new online safe havens." She added that "The Dark Web is a perfect alternative as it is inaccessible to most but navigable for the initiated few – and it is completely anonymous." reads a 2015 report published by Beatrice Berton on the use of the Darknet by ISIS.

Thomas Rid, the Professor of Security Studies at King's College London, explained that despite more than 50 percent of what's hosted in the dark web is illegal and illegitimate, terrorists do not find anonymizing network so useful.

"Militants and extremists don't seem to find the Tor hidden services infrastructure very useful. So there are few jihadist and militants in the Darknet. It's used for criminal services, fraud, extreme, illegal pornography, cyber-attacks and computer crime." said Rid.

Anyway it is essential to monitor the use of Dark web by terrorists, anonymizing networks offers a privileged environments for extremists and cybercriminals.

Hacking the Tor Network

Intelligence and law enforcement agencies worldwide face several problems when try to track users on darknets, especially the Tor network.

In February 2016, the FBI Director at the time, James Comey, publicly admitted on many occasions the difficulties faced by law enforcement when dealing with encryption during their investigations.

The FBI requested for budget for 2017, in particular asking more economic resources to break encryption when needed.

Giving a look at the FBI's Fiscal Year 2017 Budget Request document it is possible to find a specific session titled "Going Dark" that reports the following text:

"Going Dark: $38.3 million and 0 positions The requested funding will counter the threat of Going Dark, which includes the inability to access data because of challenges related to encryption, mobility, anonymization, and more. The FBI will develop and acquire tools for electronic device analysis, cryptanalytic capability, and forensic tools. Current services for this initiative are 39 positions (11 agents) and 31.0 million."

The FBI asked for $38.3 more million on top of the $31 million already requested in 2015 (a total of $69.3 million) to improve its capabilities to get encrypted data and de-anonymize Internet users.

These numbers demonstrate a significant effort of law enforcement to overwhelm the "going dark" problem.

Unmasking the Tor users is crucial for law enforcment that intend to investigate criminals that use the infrastructure for anonymizing network for illicit activities.

Across the yeas, government cyber spies and researchers have invested a considerable effort to compromise Tor infrastructure and break the encryption used to protect the traffic from prying eyes and hide the users's identity.

Organizations for the defense of online privacy and freedom of expression sustain that Governments are trying to de-anonymize Tor users to extend massive surveillance programs, their activities represent a serious threat for digital activists, whistleblowers, journalists and many other categories of individuals that use anonymizing networks to bypass the Internet.

Let's see which are the technique proposed by the experts to try to de-anonymize the Tor users

The Traffic correlation Attack

One of the first studies on the techniques to de-anonymize the Tor network was published in September 2013, by a team of researchers from Georgetown University and the US Naval Research Laboratory (USNRL) led by Aaron Johnson.

The research demonstrated how it is possible to track Tor users with a technique dubbed "Correlation Attack."

The one-year study is detailed in a paper entitled "Users Get Routed: Traffic Correlation on Tor by Realistic Adversaries", the researchers explained how a persistent adversary can monitor the user's traffic as it enters and leaves the Tor network revealing user's identity.

The technique is based on the observation and correlation of the traffic at separate locations in the network by taking advantage of identifying traffic patterns. Using the Traffic Correlation technique a persistent attacker like a government can identify the user and his traffic with the support of an internet service provider.

The paper highlights the capability of such kind of attacker that is able to control more autonomous systems (ASs),or Internet exchange point (IXPs). An attacker in this position could run a traffic correlation attack for malicious purposes with a serious impact on the user's anonymity and security.

The group of researchers assumes that the adversary has access either to Internet exchange ports, or controls a number of Autonomous Systems, a raealistic scenario that sees a law enforcement agency conducting an investigation with the help of an ISP.

"To quantify the anonymity offered by Tor, we examine path compromise rates and how quickly extended use of the anonymity network results in compromised paths", "Tor users are far more susceptible to compromise than indicated by prior work" is reported in the paper.

The team of researchers designed a tool, dubbed TorPS simulator to analyze the traffic correlation in the live TOR network, the application simulates path selection within the Tor network. The experts used the tool to demonstrate that, under certain conditions, it is possible to identify a Tor user with a 95 percent certainty. The experts explained that BitTorrent users are more exposed to the risk of identification.

"An adversary that provides no more bandwidth than some volunteers do today can deanonymize any given user within three months of regular Tor use with over 50 percent probability and within six months with over 80 percent probability. We observe that use of BitTorrent is particularly unsafe, and we show that long-lived ports bear a large security cost for their performance needs. We also observe that the Congestion-Aware Tor proposal exacerbates these vulnerabilities," the paper states.

"Tor is known to be insecure against an adversary that can observe a user's traffic entering and exiting the anonymity

network. Quite simple and efficient techniques can correlate traffic at these separate locations by taking advantage of identifying traffic patterns" "As a result, the user and his destination may beidentified, completely subverting the protocol's security goals" added the researchers.

The results were surprising, nearly 80 percent of Tor users may be deanonymized by a moderateTor-relay adversary within six months, but is the attacker is in position to manage a single AS then the technique allows to unmask 100 percent of users in some common locations in a three-month period. If the attacker is able to access only a single IXP the percentage decrease to 95 percent in a in a three-month period.

Controlling two AS, the traffic correlation technique is much more effective, the median time to deanonimize is reduced to only one day for a typical web user and from over three months to roughly one month for a BitTorrent user.

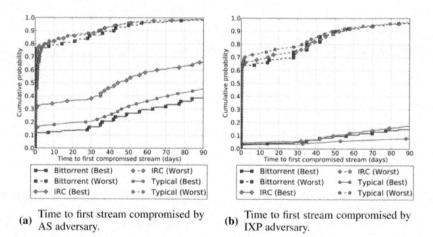

(a) Time to first stream compromised by AS adversary.

(b) Time to first stream compromised by IXP adversary.

Figure 56 - Traffic correlation attack test results

This study was one of the first analysis that demonstrated the Tor routing is exposed to traffic correlation attack.

The Confirmation attack technique

In July 2014, members of the Tor project warned Tor users about the presence of a critical vulnerability that was probably being exploited by threat actors to de-anonymize the Tor users. Early July, a group of relays was targeted by hackers that were trying to deanonymize users, as confirmed by members of the Tor project in a security advisory. The attackers were modifying Tor protocol headers to track the Tor user. The experts at the Tor project noticed that threat actors were using a technique known as "confirmation attack" to target Tor relays and unmack users accessing the Tor network.

"They appear to have been targeting people who operate or access Tor hidden services. The attack involved modifying Tor protocol headers to do traffic confirmation attacks."

The bad actors were leveraging a critical flaw in Tor to modify protocol headers in order to perform a traffic confirmation attack and inject a special code into the protocol header used to compare certain metrics from relays with the purpose to de-anonymize users.

In a traffic confirmation attack scenario, the attacker controls, or observes, the relays on both ends of a Tor circuit. The attacker analyzing some traffic characteristics, including traffic timing and volume, is able discover if two relay servers are part of the same circuit used by the stream of data from the sender to the receiver. If the first relay in the circuit (so-called the "entry guard" or "entry node") knows the IP address of the sender, and the last relay in the circuit (called "exit node") knows the resource or destination he is accessing, then the availability of these information couls allow a persistent attacker to deanonymize the user who originated the data flow.

Professor Xinwen Fu from University of Massachusetts Lowell and his team described the attack technique in a paper presented in 2009 at the US Black Hat conference. The experts described an active attack scenario that allows traffic confirmation in Tor, Xinwen dubbed the technique "replay attack", it can confirm the communication relationship in an accurate way and very quickly.

Let's see how it works, introducing the components of the Tor network involved in an ordinary connection:

- *Client*: the software used by the user to access the Tor network
- *Server*: the target TCP applications such as web servers
- *Tor (onion) router*: the special proxy relays the application data
- *Directory server*: servers holding Tor router information

Each circuit in a Tor network is built incrementally hop by hop, the sender negotiates an AES key with each router and messages are divided into segments having equal size, called the cells. Each router has a limited visibility on the message routing, it knows in fact, only its predecessor and the successor. The Exit router, is the unique server that can access to the message, but it ignores its origin.

In a replay attack scheme, the attacker uses a malicious entry onion router that duplicates cells of a message from a sender. The cell and its copy, the duplicate, traverse a series of onion routers in the network and arrive to an exit onion router along a circuit.

The presence of duplicates cause "cell recognition errors" at middle servers and at the exit router.

"Since Tor uses the counter mode AES (AES-CTR) for encryption of cells, the duplicate cell disrupts the normal counter at middle and exit onion routers and the decryption at the exit onion router incurs cell recognition errors." states Xinwen in the paper that explains the attack.

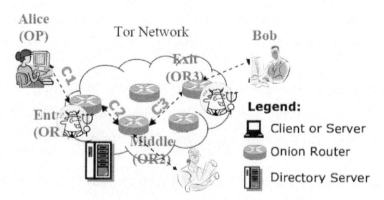

Figure 57 - Replay attack scheme

If the attacker is able to control the malicious entry router and the exit onion router, he is able to detect decryption errors and discovery the relationship between the sender and receiver.

The principal limitation of this attack is that modifying data, in many cases will cause the interruption of the connection, this make the technique very noisy and easy to be detected. Anyway, the technique could be also used to run a denial of service attack which cause the interruption of the connection due to the decryption errors.

A second limitation for this attack is that the attackers in order to run the offensive needs to control both relays, entry and exit nodes.

In the attack observed in July 2014, the attackers controlled 115 malicious fast non-exit relays, that represented a significant portion of the overall servers at the time in the Tor network (6.4 percent). As explained by the researchers at the

Tor project the servers were actively monitoring the relays on both ends of a Tor circuit in an effort to de-anonymize users.

The attackers used an active confirmation technique, so called because the entry relay injects a token into the Tor protocol headers, and then the exit relay detects and reads it.

The way they injected the signal was by sending sequences of "relay" vs "relay early" commands in the stream of data belonging to the same circuit

The malicious relays were running Tor version 50.7.0.0/16 or 204.45.0.0/16 and the attackers were using these servers to de-anonymize Tor users who visit and run so-called hidden services.

Security experts reported a security flaw in Tor, coded as CVE-2014-5117, which was exploited by remote attackers to conduct traffic confirmation attacks.

The investigation conducted by the Tor project members revealed that the relays used in the attacks joined the Tor network on January 30th 2014, in response to the attack the Tor Project team removed them on July4th 2014.

The members of Tor project also advised hidden service operators to change the location of their hidden service to avoid the localization of their infrastructure.

"While we don't know when they started doing the attack, users who operated or accessed hidden services from early February through July 4 should assume they were affected," state researchers at Tor Project.

According to members of the Tor project, the attackers were looking for users who fetched hidden service descriptors, this means that they were not able to see pages loaded by users neither whether users visited the hidden service they looked up.

"The attack probably also tried to learn who published hidden service descriptors, which would allow the attackers to learn the location of that hidden service. In theory the attack could also be used to link users to their destinations on normal Tor circuits too, but we found no evidence that the attackers operated any exit relays, making this attack less likely. And finally, we don't know how much data the attackers kept, and due to the way the attack was deployed (more details below), their protocol header modifications might have aided other attackers in deanonymizing users too." states the security advisory.

From Magneto attack to the Network Investigative Technique (NIT) script

Across the years, law enforcment adopted several techniques to attempt to de-anonymize Tor users, including malware, or exploits for flaws in the Tor browser.

In July 2013, security researchers discovered a malicious script that took advantage of a Firefox Zero-day to identify some users.

Security experts speculated that the FBI exploited the vulnerability that was present in the Firefox 17 version (MFSA 2013-53) to track Tor users. Law enforcement was stealthy implanting a tracking cookie, which fingerprinted users through a specific external server.

"Security researcher Nils reported that specially crafted web content using the onreadystatechange event and reloading of pages could sometimes cause a crash when unmapped memory is executed. This crash is potentially exploitable."

The code used to track Tor users, the Exploit code, was published online by Mozilla and the Deobfuscated JS used by the Tor Browser exploit posted on Google Code.

The exploit was based on a Javascript that is a tiny Windows executable hidden in a variable dubbed "Magneto".

The Magneto code was able to gather infromation from the the user's computer, including Windows hostname, the IP and MAC addresses and send the collected data back to a server managed by the FBI that was located in Virginia.

The script sends the machine information back the control server, outside the Tor Network, through a standard HTTP web request outside the Tor Network.

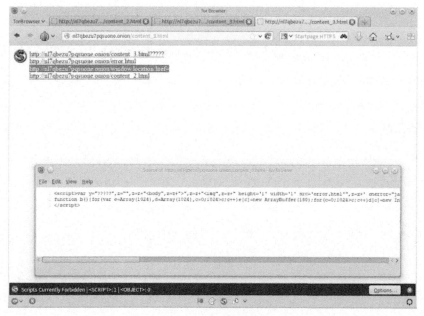

Figure 58 - The Magneto attack

The developer of the exploit, Vlad Tsyrklevich, who analyzed the malicious JavaScript code discovered that it attempted to contact a server to transfer the information related to the targeted PC.

"Briefly, this payload connects to 65.222.202.54:80 and sends it an HTTP request that includes the host name (via gethostname()) and the MAC address of the local host (via calling SendARP on gethostbyname()->h_addr_list). After that it cleans up the state and appears to deliberately crash."

The code is the first sample captured in the wild of the FBI's "computer and internet protocol address verifier," also known as CIPAV, the law enforcement spyware that was first reported by the WIRED magazine in a post dated 2007.

"Court documents and FBI files released under the FOIA have described the CIPAV as software the FBI can deliver through a browser exploit to gather information from the target machine and send it to an FBI server in Virginia. The FBI has been using the CIPAV since 2002 against hackers, online sexual predator, extortionists and others, primarily to identify suspects who are disguising their location using proxy servers or anonymity services, like Tor." reported Wired post.

In order to spread the malicious code, law enforcement used a popular hosting provider operating on the Tor network, Freedom Hosting.

On August 5th, 2013 Eric Eoin Marques, founder of Freedom Hosting, was arrested by the US law enforcement. It has been estimated that Freedom Hosting was the most popular hosting provider at the time, it was hosting nearly 50% of all Tor hidden services.

Marques was arrested on a Maryland warrant after around a year of intense investigation, the law enforcement believes that the man is "the largest facilitator of child porn on the planet."

With Marques arrest, many popular websites on the Tor Network resulted no more accessible, including popular services like Tor Mail, HackBB and the Hidden Wiki that were all hosted on Freedom Hosting. "The current news indicates that someone has exploited the software behind Freedom Hosting. From what is known so far, the breach was used to configure the server in a way that it injects some sort of javascript exploit in the web pages delivered to users. This exploit is used to load a malware payload to infect users' computers. The malware payload could be trying to exploit potential bugs in Firefox 17 ESR, on which our Tor Browser is based. We're investigating these bugs and will fix them if we can." revealed Andrew Lewman, Tor Project's Executive Director said in a blog post.

The cyber experts working for the law enforcement injected the code in the HTML of the pages visited by victims.

Once a user visited a websites containing the tracking code, the script first determined the version of the user's browser and if the user was using a vulnerble Firefox 17, then it collected the above information.

Shortly after Marques' arrest all of the hidden service sites hosted by Freedom Hosting began displaying a "Down for Maintenance" message, but some users noticed the presence of a malicious script in the source code of the maintenance page. The page was including a hidden iframe tag that loaded a collection of Javascript code from a Verizon Business internet address located in eastern Virginia.

After further investigations, security experts linked the IP address of the server used to collect data, to the National Security Agency (NSA). This revelation has been done by Baneki Privacy Labs, a collective of Internet security researchers, and VPN provider Cryptocloud.

Figure 59 - NSA Intelligence hacking catalog

"Initial investigations traced the address to defense contractor SAIC, which provides a wide range of information technology and C4ISR (Command, Control, Communications, Computers, Intelligence, Surveillance, and Reconnaissance) support to the Department of Defense. The geolocation of the IP address corresponds to an SAIC facility in Arlington, Virginia. Further analysis using a DNS record tool from Robotex found that the address was actually part of several blocks of IP addresses permanently assigned to the NSA. This immediately spooked the researchers. "One researcher contacted us and said, 'Here's the Robotex info. Forget that you heard it from me,'" a member of Baneki who requested he not be identified told Ars." revealed a post published on ArsTechnica

A few months later, On December 22nd, 2014 Mr. Joseph Gross retained the assistance of Dr. Ashley Podhradsky, Dr. Matt Miller, and Mr. Josh Stroschein to provide the testimony as the expert in the process against pedo's on Tor. The suspects were accused in federal court in Omaha of viewing and possessing of child pornography. The case assumes a particular interest because the investigators were informed about the usage of an FBI's "Network Investigative Technique" (NIT) to deanonymize suspects while accessing hidden services in the Tor network. The NIT allowed them to identify the IP address of TOR users.

"The NIT was a Flash based application that was developed by H.D.Moore and was released as part of Metasploit. The NIT, or more formally, Metaspolit Decloaking Engine was designed to provide the real IP address of web users, regardless of proxy settings." states the forensic report.

According to court documents, the investigators were informed that there were three servers containing contraband images that the FBI found and took offline in November of 2012.

The FBI decided to use the server as a bait for online pedos, then the Bureau placed the NIT on the servers and used them to de-anonymize TOR users accessing the illegal content. With this technique the FBI identified the IP addresses of visitors.

Is the NIT really effective for the identification of the Tor users?

Joe Gross challenged the accuracy of the NIT and invited the investigators verify the accuracy of the method.

On January 7th, 2015 the three experts Ashley, Matt and Josh started their investigation to test the accuracy of the NIT. The court requested them to:

- Understand the functionality of the NIT.
- Identify whether the scientific technique can be or has been tested.
- Identify whether the theory or technique has been subjected to peer review.
- Identify if there is a known rate of error for this technique.
- Identify whether the technique is generally accepted in the scientific or technical field to which it belongs.

"The investigators were given access to the NIT, decompiled the program, analyzed the code, and then verified the application output and functionality through dynamic testing of the actual application in a virtual environment. The results of

this analysis show that the NIT produced the following output from interaction with a client: IP address through the TCP connection, operating system, CPU architecture and session identification. The researchers were able to determine that if a TOR browser accessing the FBI controlled website had proper up-to-date controls configured the NIT would not be able to reveal the true IP address of the users. On the other side, if users were using the current version of the TOR browser their true IP would not be revealed. The investigators believe that the NIT provided a repeatable and reliable process of identifying true IP addresses."

The final report was issued in the mid-January 2015 and after analysis Mr. Cottom had further technical question about the NIT.

"The investigators turned in their final report mid-January and after analysis Mr. Cottom had further questions about the network and logging environment of the NIT. Mr. Cottom also switched legal representation from Mr. Joseph Gross of Timmermier, Gross and Prentiss to Mr. Joseph Howard of DLT Lawyers."

In July 2016, at least two individuals from New York have been charged with online child pornography crimes after visiting a hidden service on the Tor network. The Federal Bureau of Investigation (FBI) had used a hacking tool to identify de-anonymize the suspects while surfing on the Tor network.

More than one year later, further details about the operation were disclosed, the FBI hacked over a thousand computers, according to court documents reviewed by Motherboard.

This case is very important because it represent the first case the feds conducted a so extended operation against Tor users.

According to the court documents, the FBI monitored a bulletin board hidden service launched in August 2014, named Playpen, mainly used for "the advertisement and distribution of child pornography."

The Playpen hidden service reached in one year over 200,000 users, with over 117,000 total posts mainly containing child pornography content. The law enforcement discovered nearly 1300 IP addresses belonging to the visitors.

communications of users of "Website A." Before, during, and after its seizure by law enforcement, law enforcement agents viewed, examined and documented the contents of "Website A." Approximately 1300 true internet protocol (IP) addresses were identified during this time, one of which was user name, "xxxxoil" (the complete user name has been redacted, but is known to your affiant) operating on IP address 73.20.54.250.

Figure 60 - Court Document

According to Motherboard, the server running Playpen was seized by the FBI from a web host in North Carolina, then the law enforcement managed the computer to track its visitors. The agents used the a network investigative technique (NIT) to obtain the IP addresses of the Playpen users.

The NIT was also used in 2011, by agents running the "Operation Torpedo," it was the first time that FBI deployed a tracking code broadly against every visitor to a website, instead of targeting a particular user.

According to some clues emerged in the Playpen case, the version of NIT currently used by the FBI is different from the one used in the past during the Operation Torpedo.

The legal counsel for one of the men accused speculates that the number of individuals charged with online child pornography crimes after visiting PlayPen may increase in the next months.

"Fifteen-hundred or so of these cases are going to end up getting filed out of the same, underlying investigation," Colin Fieman, a federal public defender handling several of the related cases, told Motherboard in a phone interview. Fieman, who is representing Jay Michaud, a Vancouver teacher arrested in July 2015, said his estimate comes from what "we've seen in terms of the discovery."

"There will probably be an escalating stream of these [cases] in the next six months or so," said Colin Fieman, the federal public defender of Jay Michaud in a phone interview with Motherboard. "There is going to be a lot in the pipeline."

Deanonymizing Tor users with the analysis of DNS traffic from Tor exit relays

In 2016, a group of researchers at the Princeton University, Karlstad University and KTH Royal Institute of Technology devised two new correlation attack techniques to deanonymize Tor users.

Experts pointed out that low-latency anonymity networks such as Tor cannot protect against so-called global passive adversaries that are able to monitor both network traffic that enters and exits the network.

"While the use of Tor constitutes a significant privacy gain over off-the-shelf web browsers, it is no panacea, and the Tor Project is upfront about its limitations.

These limitations are not news to the research community. It is well understood that low-latency anonymity networks such as Tor cannot protect against so-called global passive adversaries." says Phillip Winter, a researcher at Princeton University that was involved in the research.

"We define such adversaries as those with the ability to monitor both network traffic that enters and exits the network."

The techniques were dubbed DefecTor by the researchers, they leverage on the observation of the DNS traffic from Tor exit relays, for this reason, the methods could integrate existing attack strategies.

"We show how an attacker can use DNS requests to mount highly precise website fingerprinting attacks: Mapping DNS traffic to websites is highly accurate even with simple techniques, and correlating the observed websites with a website fingerprinting attack greatly improves the precision when monitoring relatively unpopular websites. " reads the analysis published by the researchers."

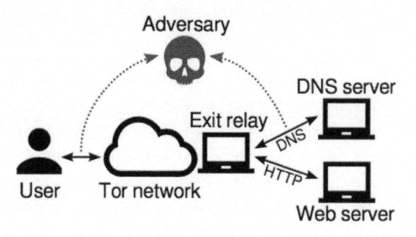

Figure 61 - Deanonymizing Tor users with the analysis of DNS traffic from Tor exit relays

The results of the test conducted by the team on the DefecTor technique are excellent, but experts explained that such attacks request a significant effort, only a persistent attacker like a government body is able to carry on such kind of offensive.The researchers were able to identify the vast majority of the visitors to unpopular visited sites using the two techniques.

"Our results show that DNS requests from Tor exit relays traverse numerous autonomous systems that subsequent web traffic does not traverse. We also find that a set of exit relays, at times comprising 40% of Tor's exit bandwidth, uses Google's public DNS servers—an alarmingly high number for a single organization. We believe that Tor relay operators should take steps to ensure that the network maintains more diversity into how exit relays resolve DNS domains." Winter added.

The experts highlighted that Google operates public DNS servers that observe almost 40% of all DNS requests exiting the Tor network, a circumstance that gives the tech giant a privileged point of observation to powet the attacks devised by the researchers. Google is also able to monitor some network traffic that is entering the Tor network, the experts reported as an example the traffic via Google Fiber or via guard relays that are occasionally running in Google's cloud. The researchers also remark that DNS requests could be used to obtain other precious information about the traffic of Tor users, they traverse autonomous systems and Internet exchanges.

"there are entities on the Internet such as ISPs, autonomous systems, or Internet exchange points that can monitor some DNS traffic but not web traffic coming out of the Tor network and potentially use the DNS traffic to deanonymize Tor users." says Winter.

"Past traffic correlation studies have focused on linking the TCP stream entering the Tor network to the one(s) exiting the network. We show that an adversary can also link the associated DNS traffic, which can be exposed to many more autonomous systems than the TCP stream."

The reaserch team developed a tool, dubbed "DNS Delegation Path Traceroute" (dptr), that could be used to determine the DNS delegation path for a fully qualified domain name. The tool runs UDP traceroutes to all DNS servers on the path that are then compared to a TCP traceroute to the web server behind the same fully qualified domain name. Just after the presentation of the results of the study conducted by the researchers, experts at the Tor Project implemented a series of major improvements to the popular anonymizing network.

In order to prevent DefecTor attacks, Tor relay operators have to ensure that the network maintains more diversity in how exit relays resolve DNS domains.

In November 2014, a team of researchers presented the results of a study coducted between 2008 and 2014 on the de-anonymization of the Tor users. The research team, led by professor Sambuddho Chakravarty has published numerous papers on the topic over the past years. Chakravarty claims that his team has reached a 100 percent 'decloaking' success rate under laboratory conditions. The research revealed that more than 81 percent of Tor clients can be de-anonymized by exploiting the Netflow technology designed by Cisco for its network appliances.

The Netflow technology was introduced by Cisco into its routers to implement an instrument to collect IP network traffic as it enters or exits an interface. The data provided by NetFlow allows a network administrator to qualify the network traffic managed by the router and identify the causes of congestion. The runs today by default in the hardware of many other network device manufacturers.

The technique proposed by Chakravarty implements an active traffic analysis based on the introduction of specific traffic perturbations on server side and evaluating a similar perturbation on the client side through statistical correlation.

"We present an active traffic analysis method based on deliberately perturbing the characteristics of user traffic at the server side, and observing a similar perturbation at the client side through statistical correlation." states the paper.

"We evaluate the accuracy of our method using both in-lab testing, as well as data gathered from a public Tor relay serving hundreds of users. Our method revealed the actual sources of anonymous traffic with 100% accuracy for the in-lab tests, and achieved an overall accuracy of about 81.4% for the real-world experiments, with an average false positive rate of 6.4."

In a previous research Chakravarty demonstrated that having access to a few Internet exchange points is enough for monitoring a significant percentage of the network paths from Tor nodes to destination servers. This means that a powerful and persistent attacker can run traffic analysis attacks by observing similar traffic patterns at various points of the network. This 2014 research revealed how to run an effective traffic analysis attack on a large scale with less traffic monitoring capabilities, such as data from Cisco's NetFlow. Unlike previous researches, this new traffic analysis attack would not necessarily need the resources of a Government to run the monitoring activity, the researcher explained that a single AS (Autonomous System) could monitor more than 39 percent of randomly-generated Tor circuits.

A traffic analysis attack exploits one or more high-bandwidth and high-performance Tor relays. The team used a modified public Tor server, hosted at the Columbia University, for its tests.

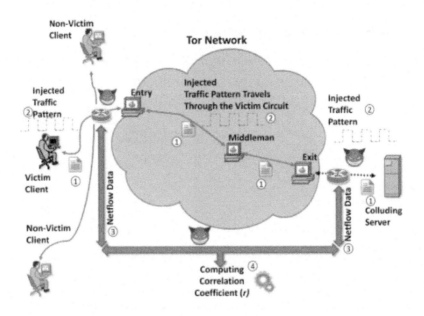

Fig. 2. Overall Process for NetFlow Based Traffic Analysis Against Tor The client downloads a file from the server ①, while the server injects a traffic pattern into the TCP connection it sees arising from the exit node ②. After a while, the connection is terminated and the adversary obtains flow data corresponding to the server to exit and entry node to client traffic ③, and computes the correlation coefficient between the server to exit traffic and entry to client statistics ④.

Figure 62 - NetFlow based traffic analysis

The researchers simulated the internet activity of a typical Tor user, they injected a repeating traffic pattern (i.e. HTML files) into the TCP connection that it sees originating in the target exit node, and then analyzed the traffic at exit node, as derived from the router's flow records, to improve client identification.

In a first phase the research was conducted in Lab environment with surprising results, in a second phase the team started the live sessions using real Tor traffic. The team

174

analyzed the traffic obtained from its public Tor relay that served hundreds of Tor circuits simultaneously.

The targeted victims were hosted on three different locations on the Planetlab, the global research network that supports the development of new network services. The chosen locations were Texas (US), Leuven (Belgium) and Corfu (Greece).

The victim clients downloaded a large file from the server that deliberately introduced perturbations in the arriving TCP connection's traffic, thereby deliberately injecting a traffic pattern in the stream between the server and the exit node.

"The process was terminated after a short while and we computed the correlation between the bytes transferred between the server and the recently terminated connection from the exit node and the entry node and the several clients that used it, during this interval." continues the paper.

The test session was organized in two parts, a first session to evaluate the effectiveness when retrieving data from open-source NetFlow packages, in the second round the researchers used sparse data obtained from its institutional Cisco router.

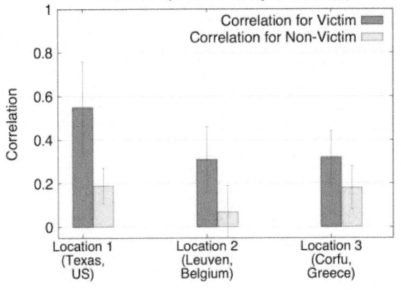

Figure 63 - Test results

Hacking communities in the Deep Web

The role of hackers has changed over the years, in the past these professionals were considered as dangerous criminals that needed to be kept at arm's length, meanwhile today they are highly sought from private companies, intelligence agencies and also by criminal gangs.

Hacking services are among the most attractive commodities in the cyber crime underground, crooks and users can hire a hacker to execute a "realistic" penetration test, or pay to take over a Gmail or Facebook account for cyber espionage purpose.

How much cost hacking services? How to hire a hacker?

Recently, journalists at Business Insider have published a post that described the prices for principal hacking services that it is possible to acquire online. According the Business Insider an individual that wants to hack someone's Gmail account will have to pay about $90.

"Hacking a Gmail address can come in handy if you lose your account password, manage other people's business accounts or simply want to improve your computer skills. " states the post. "'If you want to crack Gmail passwords, you can hack Gmail with browser settings, phishing and keylogging software and special scripts'"

A hacker could be hired to hack into a social media account, the cost to hack into someone's Facebook account is $350, or simply to increase the rank of a company on a social network.

The investigation conducted by the journalists revealed that a hacker can steal someone's Hilton HHonor points for $15 or compromise a NetFlix account just for $1.25.

Other commodities in the hacking underground are the hacking courses that goes for $20 and hit-and-run attacks, such as a DDoS or a website defacement.

"Website hack or ddos. Paying well." is the message of a hacker that promise to hack a WordPress-built website down for "2k euro."

There are various ways to buy hacking services and probably the most interesting place where it is possible to meet members of the principal hacking communities is the Dark Web ... let's explore it!

Diving in the hacking communities

The number of Hacking communities in the Deep Web is very high as reported by several investigations published by security firms and cyber experts, hackforum, Trojanforge, Mazafaka, dark0de and the TheRealDeal are just a few examples of hacking communities and black marketplaces that have grown over the time.

The majority of the hacking communities is closed to the public and request an invitation to join the discussions, in many cases, these groups focus their activities on specific topics and practices (e.g. Malware development, Social media hacking, data theft, malware and exploits and hit-and-run attacks (i.e. DDoS, Web site hacking).

Among the communities accessible only by invitation there are several hackforums, an example is the popular Trojanforge which is specialized in malware and code reversing.

Let's start our tour on the Deep Web from the results of a study conducted by the experts at Dell Secure Works Counter Threat Unit (CTU) to see what is changing from the publishing of the report and which are the dynamics and trends behind the hacking communities in the underground.

In 2013, experts at Dell Secure Works Counter Threat Unit (CTU) published a very interesting report titled "The Underground Hacking Economy is Alive and Well.," which investigated the online marketplace for stolen data and hacking services. The study listed the goods sold in the black markets and related costs. One year later, the same team of researchers at Dell SecureWorks released an update to the study of black hat markets, titled "Underground Hacker Markets", which reports a number of noteworthy trends.

The researchers observed a growing interest in the personal data, in particular in any kind of documentation that could be used as a second form of authentication, including passports, driver's licenses, Social Security numbers and even utility bills.

"The markets are booming with counterfeit documents to further enable fraud, including new identity kits, passports, utility bills, social security cards and driver's licenses." states the report.

Another distinguishing element of the evolution of the underground marketplaces in the last years was the offer of

Hacker Tutorials, as we have seen this kind of product still represents an element of attraction in the hacking community.

Training tutorials provide technical information to wannabe criminals and hackers that desire to enter into the cybercrime arena.

Online there are training on cashout of stolen credit card data, information on running exploit kits, guides for the organization of a spam and phishing campaign, and tutorials on how to organize hit-and-run DDoS attacks.

"These tutorials not only explain what a Crypter, Remote Access Trojan (RAT) and exploit kit is but also how they are used, which are the most popular, and what hackers should pay for these hacker tools," the report said.

Other tutorials offered in the hacking communities include instruction to hack ATM and to manage a network of money mules, which are the principal actors for the cash out process of every illegal activity.

The results of the investigation conducted by the experts at Dell confirmed the trends that we are assisting today. The number of data breaches continues to increase, on a daily bases fresh records and PII data flood the criminal underground.

The business model that most of all is having success is the crime-as-a-service, skilled cybercriminals offers products, services and tutorials to criminals tha want joint to the cybercrime ecosystem.

Hacking communities are very active in selling stolen credit cards, differentiating their offer to reach a wider audience and provide tailored services at higher prices.

"It is apparent that the underground hackers are monetizing every piece of data they can steal or buy and are continually adding services so other scammers can successfully carry out online and in-person fraud," states the report.

In the following table that I have found on Twitter are listed the services and the products with related prices expressed in both Bitcoin and Euro.

The prices can give us an idea about the offer of hacking service in the underground, while the prices as we have explained in this book are varying and depend on several factors, including the geographic location of the community.

Recent prices from the black market		Price	
		1BTC	213,200 EUR

N	SERVICES	BTC	EUR
50.000	Root shell	1,85	394,62
45.000	Wordpress admin passwords	1,50	319,80
50.000	SSH sniffer logs	1,20	255,84
1.000	Linux botnet	2,00	426,40
1.103.504	FTP/SSH passwords	3,00	639,60

N	SERVICES	BTC	EUR
1	Start your own maket	33,48	7.137,00
1	Virtual credit card + bank account	0,01	2,69
1	Unlimited REAL code signing	4,20	895,44

TYPE	KIT	BTC	EUR
spam	Wordpress Comment Spammer + Exploit	2,50	533,00
malware	Bitcoin Ransomware	0,21	44,77
malware	Tomcat Worm	7,40	1.578,67
malware	The real GovRAT	4,50	959,40

TYPE	EXPLOIT	BTC	EUR
1day	MS15-034 Microsoft IIS Remote Code Execution	308,53	65.778,11
1day	*NEW* ring0 LPE Exploit CVE-2015-0057	48,17	10.269,84
fud	Adobe Flash < 16.0.0.296 (CVE-2015-0313)	2,50	533,00
0day	Internet Explorer <= 11	35,00	7.462,00
0day	Android WebView 0day RCE	36,50	7.781,80
0day	Linux <= 3.13.0-48 Kernel Panic	2,00	426,40

Figure 63 - Test results

Hiring Hackers in Tor network

I'm quite suspicious of the amazing number of offers from alleged hackers advertise through several hacking forums in the underground. The experts that you will find in many hacking communities could help you to run a penetration test on your website or exploit known flaws in vulnerable websites that you intent to compromise.

Let's start our tour from the "Rent-A-Hacker" website, it seems managed by a single hacker that presents himself with the following statement:

182

"Experienced hacker offering his services! (Illegal) Hacking and social engineering is my bussiness since i was 16 years old, never had a real job so i had the time to get really good at hacking and i made a good amount of money last +-20 years. I have worked for other people before, now im also offering my services for everyone with enough cash here.

The Onion URL for its website are:

- http://haker5tkaylm5jm6.onion/
- http://5eme2auqilcux2wq.onion/
- http://gepcpf7kbng5jjyg.onion/

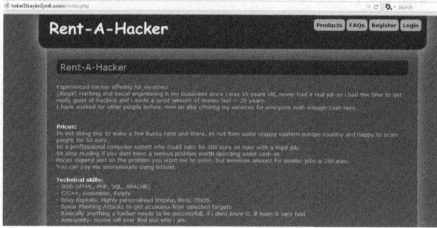

Figure 64 - Rent-A-Hacker Tor website

The hacker presents himself as a professional hacker specialized in illegal hacking services that he offer to "destroy some business or a persons' life."

Reading his description it seems to be specialized in the hacking of websites and probably he manages a botnet that it offer for rent for DDoS attacks.

The hacker explains also that he is able to run espionage campaign and tracking of pedos online. The hacker also offer services for gathering private information of any individual, every task could be committed by paying an hourly rate that is about 100 dollars, the price depend on a lot of factors, including the complexity of the task.

Product	Price
Small Job like Email, Facebook etc. hacking	200 Euro (0,95 BTC at the time I'm writing)
Medium-Large Job, ruining people, espionage, website hacking etc.	500 Euro (2,30 BTC at the time I'm writing)

Of course, the payments are anonymous and made through Bitcoin or other virtual currencies. Surfing on Tor network I have found in the past several black markets and forum offering hacking services, "Hacker for hire"(http://hacker4hhjvre2qj.onion/) was one of them. The website offered a wide range of service, from cyber frauds to hacking services. The operator of the website also offer both offensive and defensive services, specific services in fact are tailored for victims of the cybercrime.

Figure 65 - Hacker for hire Tor website

Product	Price
Hacking	
Hacking web server (vps or hosting)	USD 120 (0,49 BTC at the time I'm writing)
Hacking personal computer	USD 80 (0,49 BTC at the time I'm writing)
Security Audit	
Web Server security Audit	USD 150 (0,62 BTC at the time I'm writing)
Social media account take-over	
Social media (FB, Twitter, etc.) – account hacking	USD 50 (0,21 BTC at the time I'm writing)
Spyware and Device Tracking	
Spyware development	USD 180 (0,74 BTC at the time I'm writing)
Device Tracking	USD 60 (0,25 BTC at the time I'm writing)
Intelligence and Investigation	
Intelligent report – locate people	USD 140 (0,58 BTC at the time

	I'm writing)
Intelligent report – background checks	USD 120 (0,49 BTC at the time I'm writing)
Fraud Track – Find your Scammer	USD 120 (0,49 BTC at the time I'm writing)
Cyber extortion	To be agreed prior contact

Another website that was offering many illegal products and product was the "Hell"

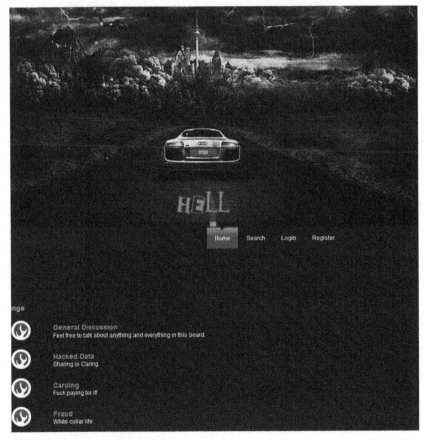

Figure 65 – The Hell hacking forum

The web portal was arranged in several sections related to hacking tools, tutorials and of course it was including the offers of many hackers. The section "Jobs" included various offers for hacking services, At the time, I contacted some of the alleged hackers negotiating the following prices for some specific tasks.

Product	Price
Hacking	
Hacking web server (vps or hosting)	USD 250 (1,04 BTC at the time I'm writing)
Hacking personal computer	USD 200 (0,83 BTC at the time I'm writing)
Hacking Social Media Account (Facebook, Twitter)	USD 300 (1,25 BTC at the time I'm writing)
Gmail Account Take over	USD 300 (1,25 BTC at the time I'm writing)
Security Audit	
Web Server security Audit	USD 400 (1,66 BTC at the time I'm writing)
Malware	
Remote Access Trojan	USD 150 - 400 (0,62 – 1,66 BTC at the time I'm writing)
Banking Malware Customization (Zeus source code)	USD 900 (3,75 BTC at the time I'm writing)
DDoS attack	
Rent a botnet for DDoS attack (24 hours)	USD 150 - 500 (2,08 – 1,66 BTC at the time I'm writing)

Even if the Tor network there are several hackers that offer their services using their own websites, black markets represent the privileged choice to get in touch with a hacker and hire him. The principal benefits to hire a hacker on a black marketplace are:

- Possibility to verify the reputation of the hacker and its abilities.
- Availability of escrow services that protect both buyers and sellers.

For this reason, I decided to explore some of the most popular black markets searching for hackers to hire.

Many of this market were recently shut down thanks to the operations conducted by law enforcement worldwide anyway the data collected at the time of the study can give us an idea of the offer in the criminal uncerground.

I started from the most popular markets such as the TheRealDeal black market.

The black market provided both sellers and buyers a privileged environment for the commercialization of exploit kits and hacking services.

Most interesting offers I have found in the listing of the market were DDoS for hire service and malware customization, along with tutorials of different kind of products and services.

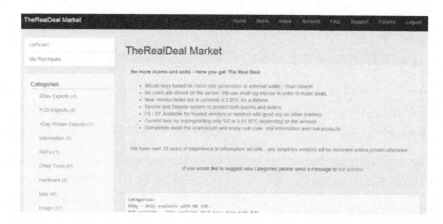

Figure 65 – The RealDeal Black market

Below a table that resume the offers I received from the hackers I contacted or that published their offers on the marketplace.

Product	Price
DDoS attack	
24 Hours DDoS Service	USD 480.61 (2 BTC at the time I'm writing)
Services	
Market set up	USD 7957.80 (33,11 BTC at the time I'm writing)
Malware	
Anonymous RAT setup for dummies	USD 1,2 (0,005 BTC at the time I'm writing)
The real GovRAT - source code + Instructions on setup and compile + 1 digital certificate for code signing to sign your files	USD 1081.38 (4,5 BTC at the time I'm writing)
RAT set up service and	USD 1201.53 (5 BTC at the time

deployment on bullet proof hosting	I'm writing)
Android RAT + Tutorial	USD 1,2 (0,005 BTC at the time I'm writing)
Hacking	
Hacking web server	USD 500 (2,08 BTC at the time I'm writing)
Hacking Social Media Account (Facebook, Twitter)	USD 200 (0,83 BTC at the time I'm writing)
Tutorial	
Hacking Tutorial, Cash out tutorial, Carding tutorial etc.	USD 2,40 - 72,09 (0,01 – 0,3 BTC at the time)

Another popular black market is Dream Market, it has reached a peak in popularity after the shut down of AlphaBay and Hansa marketplaces.

The market is more focused on products (i.e. malware, stolen card data, and fake documents) than service.

I tried to contact some members but only three of them offered me hacking services. In the following table are reported some of the products/services available on the marketplace.

Product	Price
Hacking	

Hacking Tool: Spying a Computer	USD 500 (2,08 BTC at the time I was writing)
Hacking a web server	USD 1000 (4,16 BTC at the time I was writing)
Targeted attack on a specific user	USD 2000 (8,32 BTC at the time I was writing)
Software protection cracking - Reverse engineering	USD 10 (0,04 BTC at the time I was writing)
Penetration Testing	USD 100 – 250 per hour (0,4 - 1,04 BTC at the time I was writing)
Custom Facebook Hack	USD 250 (1,04 BTC at the time I was writing)
Tutorial	
How to make a Botnet	USD 22,11 (0,09 BTC at the time I was writing)
How to set up a RAT	USD 0,11 (0,00004 BTC at the time I was writing)

Conclusions

It isn't so difficult to hire a hacker in the numerous black markets in the Dark Web, especially when someone want to assign them simple tasks. The situation is quite different when you search for a professional hacking team to hire, these groups usually use different channels to communicate with a restricted number of clients. Another consideration to make is that most of services offered through several hidden services are scams and in many cases the hackers are not able to complete their tasks.

Dark web ... not only cybercrime

It is quite easy to read about criminal activities in the Deep Web, we have described the numerous scenarios related to illegal activities that exploit anonimity offered by network such as Tor or I2P.

Anyway it is important to consider also the numerous services that ara managed for other purposes. In this paragraph we will make a rapid tour about various hidden services hosted on the Tor network that propose alternative content.

Of course the first website that comes to mind is the popular social network Facebook, the company has launched the Facebook Tor hidden service to provide a method to use its site securely. Write down the onion address!

https://facebookcorewwwi.onion/

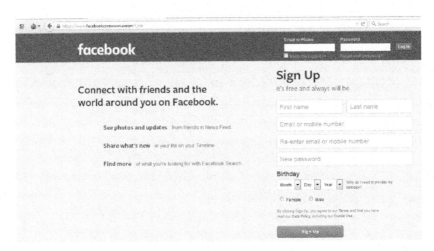

Figure 26 - Facebook Tor Hidden Service

Using the Facebook Tor hidden service, its users were able to benefit end-to-end encryption for the communications and protect them from eavesdropping and monitoring.

"we have begun an experiment which makes Facebook available directly over Tor network at the following URL: https://facebookcorewwwi.onion/ "said the company in an official announcement, Facebook makes clear that the service is in an experimental phase at the moment and that there will likely be bugs to work out.

Facebook also used an SSL certificate for the deployment of its hidden service, a measure taken by the company to avoid attack against the platform and to implemen a mutual authentication of the users once connected to the service of the social network. It is the first time that a legitimate SSL digital certificate was issued for a .onion website.

"we have provided an SSL certificate which cites our onion address; this mechanism removes the Tor Browser's "SSL Certificate Warning" for that onion address and increases confidence that this service really is run by Facebook. Issuing an SSL certificate for a Tor implementation is – in the Tor world – a novel solution to attribute ownership of an onion address; other solutions for attribution are ripe for consideration, but we believe that this one provides an appropriate starting point for such discussion."

Another interesting and useful hidden service available on the Tor network is the popular DuckDuckGo search engine.

DuckDuckGo is considered by the experts the search engine that most of all protect the user's privacy and doesn't collect information of the user's queries in order to provide personalized search results. DuckDuckGo shows all users the same search results for the same query.

It's onion addess is http://3g2upl4pq6kufc4m.onion/

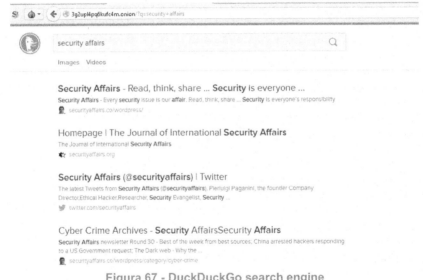

Figura 67 - DuckDuckGo search engine

Browsing the Tor network I come across an hidden service that offers music in streaming, a Deep Web radio. Who said that in the darkness of the web you do not listen to music?

http://76qugh5bey5gum7l.onion/

Figure 68 - Deep Web Radio

Just a couple of clicks and I discover a website that reports detailed information on the network of steam tunnels that run beneath much of the Virginia Tech campus. Interesting information for ill-intentioned, what do you think about?

http://74ypjqjwf6oejmax.onion/

Figura 69 - Beneath VT Steam tunnels map

Be aware you will find many stores that propose electronic equipments ad disconted prices, including iPhone and Samsung mobile devices.

Many of these website are managed by fraudsters so think twice before pay, of course by using the Bitcoin in your wallet. You will never receive the devices or in rare case your devices is used by "trustable" crooks sell devices paid with stolen card data. Below an example of hidden service used to sell mobile devices, I have no idea on the origin of the goods.

http://mobil7rab6nuf7vx.onion/

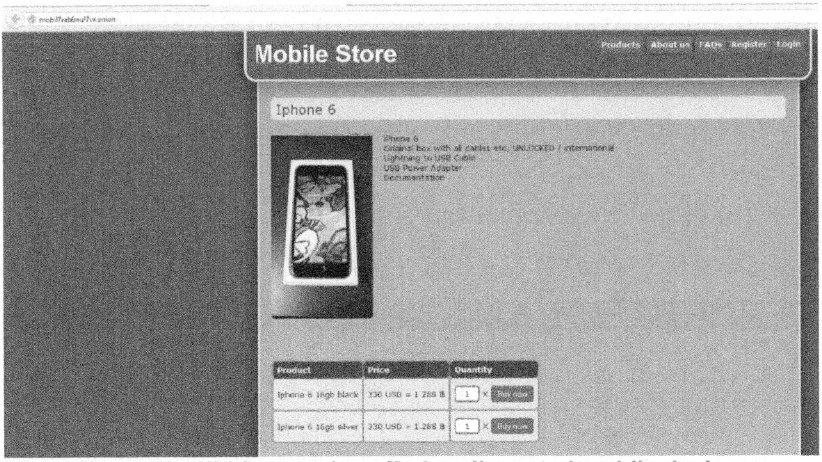

Figure 70 - Hidden service offering disconted mobile devices

Among hidden services hosted on the Tor network it is quite easy to find website offering music and books.

The following website for example allow users to upload music, all the files are grouped in categories to make easy the search of titles.

http://wuvdsbmbwyjzsgei.onion/

In my short tour I have found many websites offering books. The Imperial Library of Trantor (also known as Galactic Library) is a repository of DRM-free ebooks on ePub format.

Figure 71 - The Imperial Library of Trantor (Thriller Category)

Another website, Jotunbane's Reading Club offers any kind of books to its readers, some of them very interetsing.

http://c3jemx2ube5v5zpg.onion/

Figura 723 - Jotunbane's Reading Club

Other services very popular amont the Tor users are the Email and Messaging platfrom spefically designed to protect anonymity. The Tor Mail Box is a hidden mailbox service that is accessible only via TOR, all the emails are sent and received within TorBox.

http://torbox3uiot6wchz.onion/

Another interesting service is SMS4TOR that allows users to send self destructing messages. The user create a note and the system generate a TOR URL to share with the recipient. Once visited the TOR URL the message is display and destroyed.

https://sms4tor3vcr2geip.onion

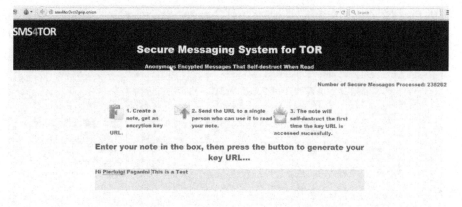

Figure 734 - SMS4TOR Messaging System

Another interesting website is " Autistici/Inventati" a collective that define itself an autonomous anticapitalist movement who fights for digital rights.

They provide a set of digital tools for privacy self-defence, including Web Hosting, Anonymity Services / Personal VPNs, and Instant Messaging and Chat.

http://wi7qkxyrdpu5cmvr.onion/

Searching for political content, The Intel Exchange Forum is one of the most popular website where to find discussions on various topics, ranging from Illegal activities to Conspiracy Theories.

http://rrcc5uuudhh4oz3c.onion

Author	Message
	7 weeks and 6 hours ago
Maly_Krtek	did you hear about that guys who will torture and kill isis members in a free live stream? http://vt2s4g732zw6ym.onion/ here is the link the stream will start at the 29. august at 00:00 utc i dont know if its fake or real and i also dont really know what to think of this :/ takedownman (yt) brought this to my attention
	6 weeks and 5 days ago
Mr.Archer47	yeah i am curious about this too, i found out about it on 8chan
	6 weeks and 5 days ago
Nix	I downloaded the first part of the stream. It's really nothing to write home about. It's impossible to identify either man from the footage so it's not really of interest to me anymore but if you care the stream is available for download in parts.
	6 weeks and 4 days ago
goliath	FBI and Homeland have took down the page. i didnt expect them to put it down this fast but i guess they had known about the page for some time now
	6 weeks and 3 days ago
Maly_Krtek	Takedownman saied the stream was fake i coldnt watch it because i was buisy

Figura 74 - The Intel Exchange Forum

200

References

Tor Metrics Web Portal (2014) - https://metrics.torproject.org/

Patrick Howell O'Neill, (2014, June 18). "As Iraq censors Internet, Tor usage jumps tenfold." The Daily Dot. Retrieved from http://www.dailydot.com/politics/iraq-internet-censorship-tor/

Deep Web Statistics (2014) - http://hewilson.wordpress.com/what-is-the-deep-web/statistics/

He, Bin, Mitesh Patel, Zhen Zhang, and Kevin Chen-Chuan Chang, (2005). "Accessing the Deep Web: A Survey." Department of Computer Science, University of Illinois.

Kunder, Maurice de. (2011, November 11). World Wide Web Size. 2011. From http://www.worldwidewebsize.com/.

ELIZABETH CLARKE - Dell (November 2013) - The Underground Hacking Economy is Alive and Well https://www.secureworks.com/blog/the-underground-hacking-economy-is-alive-and-well

Wired (2013, August)- Feds are suspects in new malware that attacks tor anonymity (2013, May) https://www.wired.com/2013/08/freedom-hosting/

Pierluigi Paganini - Infosec Institute (2017) - The Dark Web: a Paradise for Scammers http://resources.infosecinstitute.com/the-dark-web-a-paradise-for-scammers/#gref

European Central Bank - Fourth report on card fraud https://www.ecb.europa.eu/pub/pdf/other/4th_card_fraud_report.en.pdf

ArsTechnica - Update: Researchers say Tor-targeted malware phoned home to NSA https://arstechnica.com/tech-policy/2013/08/researchers-say-tor-targeted-malware-phoned-home-to-nsa/

BusinessInsider - Cale Guthrie Weissman (May 2018)

9 things you can hire a hacker to do and how much it will (generally) cost
www.businessinsider.com/9-things-you-can-hire-a-hacker-to-do-and-how-much-it-will-generally-cost-2015-5?IR=T

IntSight (2017 November) - Monetizing the Insider: The Growing Symbiosis of Insiders and the Dark Web
https://www.virtuallyinformed.com/vi-newswatch/news-watch/reports/monetizing-the-insider-the-growing-symbiosis-of-insiders-and-the-dark-web

Europol (2017 November)
Drugs and the darknet: a growing threat to health and security
http://www.emcdda.europa.eu/news/2017/18/darknet-report_en

Daniel Moore & Thomas Rid (2016) "Cryptopolitik and the Darknet"
http://www.tandfonline.com/doi/abs/10.1080/00396338.2016.1142085

Gabriel Weimann (2016) "Terrorist Migration to the Dark Web"
http://www.terrorismanalysts.com/pt/index.php/pot/article/view/513/html

Andy Greenberg (2014, December 30). "Over 80 Percent of Dark-Web Visits Relate to Pedophilia, Study Finds". From
http://www.wired.com/2014/12/80-percent-dark-web-visits-relate-pedophilia-study-finds/

Sambuddho Chakravarty, Marco V. Barbera, Georgios Portokalidis, Michalis Polychronakis, Angelos D. Keromytis (2014, November). "On the Effectiveness of Traffic Analysis Against Anonymity Networks Using Flow Records"
https://mice.cs.columbia.edu/getTechreport.php?techreportID=1545&format=pdf&

Beatrice Berton (June 2015) – "The dark side of the web: ISIL's one-stop shop?"
From
https://www.iss.europa.eu/content/dark-side-web-isil%E2%80%99s-one-stop-shop

Bergman, Michael K. (2001, August)
White Paper: The Deep Web: Surfacing Hidden Value
Journal Of Electronic Publishing. Retrieved from
http://quod.lib.umich.edu/j/jep/3336451.0007.104?view=text;rgn=main

Sambuddho Chakravarty, Marco V. Barbera, Georgios Portokalidis, Michalis Polychronakis, Angelos D. Keromytis (2014)

On the Effectiveness of Traffic Analysis Against Anonymity Networks Using Flow Records
https://mice.cs.columbia.edu/getTechreport.php?techreportID=1545&format=pdf&

Josh Pitts -The Case Of The Modified Binaries
From http://www.leviathansecurity.com/blog/the-case-of-the-modified-binaries/

Digital Citizens Alliance (2014, September) - Darknet Marketplace Watch - Monitoring Sales of Illegal Drugs on the Darknet. From
http://www.digitalcitizensalliance.org/cac/alliance/content.aspx?page=Darknet

Motherboard (January, 2016) The FBI's 'Unprecedented' Hacking Campaign Targeted Over a Thousand Computers
https://motherboard.vice.com/en_us/article/qkj8vv/the-fbis-unprecedented-hacking-campaign-targeted-over-a-thousand-computers

Security Affairs - Pierluigi Paganini (2014, September) - The rapid growth of the Darknet black markets. From
http://securityaffairs.co/wordpress/28048/cyber-crime/black-markets-growth.html

Security Affairs - Pierluigi Paganini (2014, September) - The rapid growth of the Darknet black markets. From
http://securityaffairs.co/wordpress/28048/cyber-crime/black-markets-growth.html

Security Affairs - Pierluigi Paganini (2015, July) - NIT, the Flash code the FBI used to deanonymize pedo's on Tor
http://securityaffairs.co/wordpress/38213/cyber-crime/nit-fbi-deanonymize-tor.html

Security Affairs - Pierluigi Paganini (2017, February) - Weaponizing of the insider in the Dark Web, a dangerous phenomenon
http://securityaffairs.co/wordpress/55868/deep-web/weaponizing-insider-dark-web.html

Security Affairs - Pierluigi Paganini (2014, July) - Discovered attacks to compromise TOR Network and De-Anonymize users From
http://securityaffairs.co/wordpress/27193/hacking/attacks-against-tor-network.html

Security Affairs - Pierluigi Paganini (2014, July) - Discovered attacks to compromise TOR Network and De-Anonymize users From http://securityaffairs.co/wordpress/27193/hacking/attacks-against-tor-network.html

Security Affairs - Pierluigi Paganini (2014, November) - 81 percent of Tor clients can be identified with traffic analysis attack http://securityaffairs.co/wordpress/30202/hacking/tor-traffic-analysis-attack.html

Security Affairs - Pierluigi Paganini (2016, October) - DefecTor – Deanonymizing Tor users with the analysis of DNS traffic from Tor exit relays http://securityaffairs.co/wordpress/51848/deep-web/defector-tor-deanonymizing.html

Security Affairs - Pierluigi Paganini (2016, January) - The FBI used the NIT to de-anonymize thousand Pedos on Tor http://securityaffairs.co/wordpress/43442/cyber-crime/fbi-used-nit-against-pedo.html

Tor Project (2014) - "One cell is enough to break Tor's anonymity" https://blog.torproject.org/one-cell-enough-break-tors-anonymity

Security Affairs - Pierluigi Paganini (2015) - The ISIS advances in the DeepWeb among Bitcoin and darknets From The ISIS advances in the DeepWeb among Bitcoin and darknets

Security Affairs - Pierluigi Paganini (2018, February) - Counterfeit Code-Signing certificates even more popular, but still too expensive http://securityaffairs.co/wordpress/69457/cyber-crime/code-signing-certificates-2.html

Security Affairs - Pierluigi Paganini (2018) - Counterfeit Code-Signing certificates even more popular, but still too expensive http://securityaffairs.co/wordpress/69457/cyber-crime/code-signing-certificates-2.html

Security Affairs - Pierluigi Paganini (2014, November) - 81 percent of Tor clients can be identified with traffic analysis attack. From http://securityaffairs.co/wordpress/30202/hacking/tor-traffic-analysis-attack.html

Security Affairs - Pierluigi Paganini (2014, December) - Seizure of the directory authorities could block the Tor network. From http://securityaffairs.co/wordpress/29589/cyber-crime/tor-exit-node-serves-malware.html

Security Affairs - Pierluigi Paganini (2013, September) - Traffic Correlation Attacks against Anonymity on Tor from http://securityaffairs.co/wordpress/17489/intelligence/traf%EF%AC%81c-correlation-vs-anonymity-on-tor.html

The Blog Tor Project - (2014, December) - Directory authorities - Possible upcoming attempts to disable the Tor network. From https://blog.torproject.org/category/tags/directory-authorities

Security Affairs - Pierluigi Paganini (2014, August) - A dark wing of the intelligence supports the Tor Project. From http://securityaffairs.co/wordpress/31380/hacking/directory-authorities-block-tor-network.html

Security Affairs - Pierluigi Paganini (2014, November) - Bitcoin anonymity, hackers can deanonymize users from their transactions. From http://securityaffairs.co/wordpress/27751/intelligence/intelligence-supports-tor-project.html

Security Affairs - Pierluigi Paganini (2014, November) - Russian Tor exit node patches with malware the files downloaded. From http://securityaffairs.co/wordpress/30610/hacking/bitcoin-anonymity-hacked.html

Security Affairs - Pierluigi Paganini (2014, December) - Operation Tornado – FBI Used Metasploit to unmask Tor users. From http://securityaffairs.co/wordpress/31174/cyber-crime/operation-tornado-fbi-against-tor.html

Security Affairs - Pierluigi Paganini (2017, August) - ZITiS is the new German Government cyber unit in wake of terror attacks http://securityaffairs.co/wordpress/50297/terrorism/zitis-german-cyber-unit.html

Security Affairs - Pierluigi Paganini (2017, July) - UK Police: Accessing the Darkweb could be a sign of terrorism http://securityaffairs.co/wordpress/60798/terrorism/darkweb-terrorism.html

Security Affairs - Pierluigi Paganini (2016, September) - UK Government is hiring cyber experts for Dark Web investigations http://securityaffairs.co/wordpress/62728/deep-web/uk-government-dark-web.html

Wired – Kevin Poulsen (2014, December) The FBI Used the Web's Favorite Hacking Tool to Unmask Tor Users. From
http://www.wired.com/2014/12/fbi-metasploit-tor/

Infosec Institute - Pierluigi Paganini (2014) - Hacking TOR and Online anonymity.
From http://resources.infosecinstitute.com/hacking-tor-online-anonymity/

Infosec Institute - Pierluigi Paganini (2018) – Malware in the Dark Web.
From http://resources.infosecinstitute.com/malware-dark-web/

Security Affairs - Pierluigi Paganini (2015, April) - Dark Web Email Service SIGAINT hacked by the Intelligence . From
http://securityaffairs.co/wordpress/36292/hacking/sigaint-hacked-by-intelligence.html

[tor-talk] - SIGAINT email service targeted by 70 bad exit nodes
From https://lists.torproject.org/pipermail/tor-talk/2015-April/037549.html

Security Affairs - Pierluigi Paganini (2015, January) - 83 Percent of Tor hidden service traffic flowed to Pedo websites. Study finds.
http://securityaffairs.co/wordpress/31690/cyber-crime/pedo-websites-tor-network.html

Security Affairs - Pierluigi Paganini (2015, June) - Darknets in the Deep Web, the home of assassins and pedophiles
http://securityaffairs.co/wordpress/38080/cyber-crime/deep-web-report.html

The Tor project (2014, July) - security advisory: "relay early" traffic confirmation attack (2014, July) -
From https://blog.torproject.org/blog/tor-security-advisory-relay-early-traffic-confirmation-attack

Ryan Pries, Wei Yu, Xinwen Fu and Wei Zhao (2009)
A New Replay Attack Against Anonymous Communication Networks
http://www.cs.uml.edu/~xinwenfu/paper/ICC08_Fu.pdf

Andrei Barysevich (2018)
The Use of Counterfeit Code Signing Certificates Is on the Rise
https://www.recordedfuture.com/code-signing-certificates/

Philipp Winter (2016)
The Effect of DNS on Tor's Anonymity
https://freedom-to-tinker.com/2016/09/29/the-effect-of-dns-on-tors-anonymity/

Andrei Barysevich (2018 February)
The Use of Counterfeit Code Signing Certificates Is on the Rise
https://www.recordedfuture.com/code-signing-certificates/

Alex Biryukov, Dmitry Khovratovich, Ivan Pustogarov (2014)
Deanonymisation of clients in Bitcoin P2P network
http://orbilu.uni.lu/handle/10993/18679

Xinwen Fu, Zhen Ling,Junzhou Luo,Wei Yu, Weijia Jia, Wei Zhao (2009)
One Cell is Enough to Break Tor's AnonymityFreenet and i2P
https://www.blackhat.com/presentations/bh-dc-09/Fu/BlackHat-DC-09-Fu-Break-Tors-Anonymity-slides.pdf

Security Affairs - Pierluigi Paganini (2013, September) - Traffic Correlation
Attacks against Anonymity on Tor. From:
http://securityaffairs.co/wordpress/17489/intelligence/traf%EF%AC%81c-correlation-vs-anonymity-on-tor.html

Aaron Johnson, Chris Wacek, Rob Jansen, Micah Sherr, Paul Syverson (2013)
Users Get Routed:Traffic Correlation on Tor by Realistic Adversaries
http://www.ohmygodel.com/publications/usersrouted-ccs13.pdf

Security Affairs - Pierluigi Paganini (2013, August) - Firefox Zero-day
exploited against Tor anonymity
From: http://securityaffairs.co/wordpress/16924/cyber-crime/firefox-zero-day-exploited-against-tor-anonymity.html

Security Affairs - Pierluigi Paganini (2015, December) - Inside the German
cybercriminal underground
http://securityaffairs.co/wordpress/42802/cyber-crime/german-cybercriminal-underground.html

Security Affairs - Pierluigi Paganini (2017, October) - Digging the Middle
East and North African cybercrime underground market
http://securityaffairs.co/wordpress/64649/cyber-crime/north-african-cybercrime-underground.html

Mayra Rosario Fuentes, Trend Micro (2017)
The Middle Eastern and North African Underground: Where Culture and
Cybercrime Meet
https://www.trendmicro.com/vinfo/us/security/news/cybercrime-and-digital-threats/the-middle-eastern-and-north-african-underground-where-culture-and-cybercrime-meet

Fernando Mercês, Trend Micro (2014)

The Brazilian Underground Market Fernando Mercês
https://www.trendmicro.de/cloud-content/us/pdfs/security-intelligence/white-papers/wp-the-brazilian-underground-market.pdf

Noah Gamer, Trend Micro (2015)
The North American underground – and where hackers like to hide
https://www.trendmicro.de/cloud-content/us/pdfs/security-intelligence/white-papers/wp-the-brazilian-underground-market.pdf

Security Affairs - Pierluigi Paganini (2015, December) - The North American cyber-criminal underground it's easy to access!
http://securityaffairs.co/wordpress/42663/cyber-crime/north-american-criminal-underground.html

Security Affairs - Pierluigi Paganini (2015, October) - The rise of the Japanese Cybercrime Underground
http://securityaffairs.co/wordpress/41001/cyber-crime/japanese-cybercrime-underground.html

Security Affairs - Pierluigi Paganini (2015, November) - A deep look into the Brazilian underground cyber-market
http://securityaffairs.co/wordpress/30350/cyber-crime/brazilian-underground-cyber-market.html

Security Affairs - Pierluigi Paganini (2017, November) - Experts explain the Return on Investments in the cybercriminal underground
http://securityaffairs.co/wordpress/65261/deep-web/cybercriminal-underground.html

Recorded Future (2017) - Dissecting the Costs of Cybercriminal Operations
https://www.recordedfuture.com/cyber-operations-cost/

Akira Urano - Trend Micro (2015)
The Japanese Underground
https://www.trendmicro.de/cloud-content/us/pdfs/security-intelligence/white-papers/wp-the-japanese-underground.pdf

Trend Micro (2015)
U-Markt Peering into the German Cybercriminal Underground
https://www.trendmicro.de/cloud-content/us/pdfs/security-intelligence/white-papers/wp-u-markt.pdf

Lion Gu, Trend Micro (2014) - The Chinese Underground in 2013
U-Markt Peering into the German Cybercriminal Underground

https://www.trendmicro.de/cloud-content/us/pdfs/security-intelligence/white-papers/wp-the-chinese-underground-in-2013.pdf

Security Affairs - Pierluigi Paganini (2014, August) - UK – A new GCHQ-NCA unit will catch pedophiles in the Deep Web From: http://securityaffairs.co/wordpress/31077/cyber-crime/gchq-nca-catch-pedophiles-deep-web.html

Security Affairs - Pierluigi Paganini (2014, September) - Chinese criminal underground is doubled between 2012 and 2013 http://securityaffairs.co/wordpress/28074/cyber-crime/chinese-underground.htm l

Security Affairs - Pierluigi Paganini (2017, October) - Digging the Middle East and North African cybercrime underground market. From http://securityaffairs.co/wordpress/64649/cyber-crime/north-african-cybercrime-underground.html

Security Affairs - Pierluigi Paganini (2017, February) - Weaponizing of the insider in the Dark Web, a dangerous phenomenon. From https://securityaffairs.co/wordpress/55868/deep-web/weaponizing-insider-dark-web.html

Security Affairs - Pierluigi Paganini (2017, October) - Digging the Middle East and North African cybercrime underground market. From http://securityaffairs.co/wordpress/64649/cyber-crime/north-african-cybercrime-underground.html

Trend Micro (2017) - The Middle Eastern and North African Underground: Where Culture and Cybercrime Meet.
From **Errore. Riferimento a collegamento ipertestuale non valido.** https://www.trendmicro.com/vinfo/us/security/news/cybercrime-and-digital-threats/the-middle-eastern-and-north-african-underground-where-culture-and-cybercrime-meet

Trend Micro (2017) - Russian Underground Revisited https://www.trendmicro.de/cloud-content/us/pdfs/security-intelligence/white-papers/wp-russian-underground-revisited.pdf#sf25040664

Recorded Future (2017) - Dissecting the Costs of Cybercriminal Operations.
From https://www.recordedfuture.com/cyber-operations-cost/

CSO (2015) - After Paris, ISIS moves propaganda machine to Darknet
From
https://www.csoonline.com/article/3004648/security-awareness/after-paris-isis-moves-propaganda-machine-to-darknet.html